REBELS
The Rebel Hero in Films

THE REBEL

REBELS
HERO IN FILMS

by JOE MORELLA and EDWARD Z. EPSTEIN

Introduction by JUDITH CRIST

THE CITADEL PRESS   New York

First Edition
Copyright © 1971 by Joe Morella and Edward Z. Epstein
All rights reserved
Published by Citadel Press, Inc.
A subsidiary of Lyle Stuart, Inc.
222 Park Avenue South, New York, N.Y. 10003
In Canada: George J. McLeod Limited
73 Bathurst St., Toronto 2B, Ontario
Manufactured in the United States of America
by Halliday Lithograph Corp., West Hanover, Mass.
Designed by A. Christopher Simon
Library of Congress catalog card number: 72-147827
ISBN 0-8065-0231-2

To Molly, Pat, Pat Jr., and Grams
And to Rose, Len, Vivian, Steve, and Jenny

ACKNOWLEDGMENTS

Our sincere thanks to: Columbia Pictures; Paramount Pictures; United Artists; United Artists Television; Eric Naumann, Universal Pictures; Gordon Weaver, Cinema Center Films; Paula Klaw, "Movie Star News" collection; Phyllis Schwartz; William Kenly; Stuart Byron. Grateful acknowledgment is made to Warner Bros. for the use of stills from their post–1948 films.

Thanks, too, to Patrick and Eleanor Clark, Beth Fallon, and James Bonavita.

And a very special thank you to Judith Crist and to David C. L'Heureux.

Contents

REBELS
The Rebel Hero in Films

Introduction

BY JUDITH CRIST

In the beginning the good guys in the white hats won not only the West and the local schoolteacher but also our hearts and our daydreams, and the black-hatted bad guys were, thank goodness, too stone cold dead even to mutter "Foiled again!," let alone go slinking off stage. Heroes were heroes in them days, stiff of deportment, stout of heart, neat of hair and as clean-shaven as blond virtue and frank face and contemporary coiffure allowed. They did the right thing and delivered the lawful goods in neat packages, whether it was a lady (rescued from death or a fate worse than, from a burning shack or a loveless marriage to a dirty old man, all because of daddy's unpaid mortgage), the mortgage itself (restored to daddy or, as John Wayne is still doing in 1971, returned to a passel of decent God-fearin' ranchers) or justice for the oppressed (in the city slum or the wide open space). Handsome, efficient, devoted to mom and flag and blondes (good ones; bad blondes, we suspected, turned brunette to serve as shady ladies or badmen's darlings, unless they were dumb blondes who were either comediennes or gangsters' victims or turncoat molls), the heroes of yore were straightforward, ten-hearted men, no quibbles allowed. And then....

I don't quite know whether it was the heroes who

1

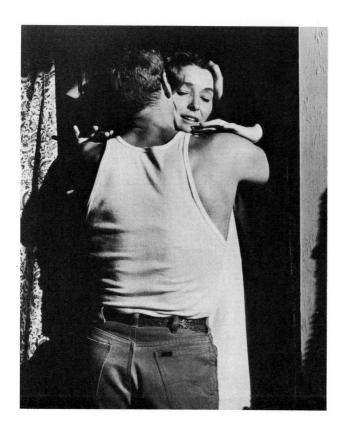

changed first or whether it was that the bad guys began to poach on their terrain. Suddenly, it seems to me, back there in the thirties the villains began sneaking into our hearts. The Cagney-type gangsters began meeting their maker on the steps of churches, shot down before a cathedral-like structure and going into a heart-rending death-crawl up toward the doorway. The Garfield-type prodigal-gone-bad would knock on the door and croak "Mom—I'm home!" and drop dead in the arms of Beryl Mercer or May Robson or some other prodigal's-mother type of the time. Who could hate such men with a whole heart? And when—unforgettably for me back in '34—Clark Gable, racketeer though he was, walked high-headed to the electric chair for killing a grafter who was trying to ruin his boyhood chum, District Attorney William Powell (Gable had also practically handed over his girl, Myrna Loy, to Powell, such was his true-blue friendship), and had refused to let Governor Powell (yes, the boyhood chum won the election after successfully prosecuting Gable) commute his sentence out of friendship—when all this came to pass, dear reader, in an item labeled *Manhattan Melodrama* and strong striplings wept with us lasses and we hated Powell for letting Gable be such a good pal, then the day of the rebel hero was upon us. Social outcasts maybe, the tough-guy Gable and the swashbuckling Errol Flynn, the *Grapes of Wrath* Fonda fresh from prison

but seeking only a human's rights, the *Algiers* Boyer leaving the thieves' den for love of lady—all gentlemen of the old school, all of them after virtue albeit seeking it from the wrong side of the moral track.

And then the hero moved into the middle of the track, given impetus by John Garfield's Depression-era embittered characters and substance by Bogart's tough cynicism of the forties. Bogart perhaps embodied the dichotomy of the breed, the man on the outside (of good or evil) knowing the rotten rules he had to follow. A bad guy? Okay—but the instincts are a good guy's and he'll leave his *High Sierra* hideout to help a crippled girl, he'll be patient with a lonely bad girl and he'll be loyal to the top crook. A good guy? He'll show his contempt for the crooks who masquerade as decent citizens and he'll shove honor down their throats, because when a man's partner is killed. . . . And here lie the roots of the young rebels of the fifties, the young men who know the score—and it's a low one in a corrupt society; they play an internal game and wear a mask.

Marlon Brando is, of course, the prototype of the vulnerable man who cares so very deeply that he must pretend to care not at all, and the not-caring is epitomized by the mumble and the inarticulate response, the hooded eye to shield the hungry heart, the hunched shoulder to hide the sensitivity of soul. Brando, Montgomery Clift, James Dean were the alienated heroes of

2

the fifties who found an empathetic response from the young audiences of that so-called silent generation and gave a life-style to the not-so-silent young of the sixties. The do-your-own-thing principle of the last decade has its seed in Clift's Prewitt, the beautiful trumpet player of *From Here to Eternity* who rejected violence and refused to conform: "If a man doesn't go his own way, he's nothin'," he declares—and the system grinds him to dust. For all the unloved, the unappreciated, the emotionally starved, there's Dean's Cal to cry out to the painted whore in *East of Eden*, "Talk to me—please—mother!" And for the shattered dream and the damaged hearts, there's Brando's "But you were my brother, Charlie!" and "I could have had class—I could have been a contender. I could have been somebody instead of a bum, which I am."

The rebel hero is never to blame for his life outside the system. Children of Freud, all of them. It was mom or dad or brother Charlie or the whole damn system that didn't care enough, that made them what they are—and we, as wonderfully passive audience, take our relief from self-realization by wallowing in their despairs. And by the time of *Hud* we were ready to accept not just the rebel but the heel as hero. Paul Newman's Texan is the man who doesn't give a damn, who's fully aware that the world's "full of crap" that contaminates everyone sooner or later; he can give with the Freud jargon

himself (daddy hates him because he caused his brother's death and "My mama loved me—but she died") and he asks for no rationales from us. Those baby blues and all-American Greek-god good looks are the front; figure out what's underneath. And if you do, you'll take off and leave him in possession.

The small-boy-innocent takeover was completed in the sixties, with the Dead End kids all grown up and psyched out and in control, courtesy of their wheels and their drug culture and their tripping. And who are we to rebel against the rebels? Like Dustin Hoffman's Graduate we know the answer isn't in one word, let alone "plastics." Like Warren Beatty's Mickey One, we face the fact that there is no word at all and that we are all "guilty of not being innocent." But perhaps we're approaching the end of easy rides with rebels when our heart isn't touched by the inarticulate "wow, man—like I mean—y'know?" of the Fondas and Hoppers, but it's shattered by the squareness and involvement of the Jack Nicholson character. We may be heading for the return of the heroic man—though I doubt that we'll spot him by his white hat this time around. And in the meantime—a sigh and a nostalgic toast to the unheroic, rebels in their time.

Foreword

What can be said about a social order that no longer accepts good and evil as absolutes? If it is difficult to distinguish between good and evil, what is the future of the hero in literature and films?

In films it has been relatively easy, until now, to identify the hero. The cinema thus far has produced three basic types of hero: traditional hero, rebel hero and anti-hero (or non-hero).

It was not until the appearance of John Garfield on the screen in 1938 that the "rebel hero" came into being, although such stars as James Cagney, Humphrey Bogart, Paul Muni, and even Clark Gable exhibited some quali-

ties of the "rebel" in certain films in the early thirties.

In *Four Daughters*, Garfield established the rebel hero character which was the basis for his entire career and which paved the way for the screen rebel type and it has evolved for the past three decades—from Garfield to Montgomery Clift, Marlon Brando, James Dean, Paul Newman, Steve McQueen, Warren Beatty, Dustin Hoffman, and Peter Fonda. This book will be concerned with these "rebel hero" stars.

Before Garfield, men of the screen had been either good or evil. There was a clear-cut distinction as to hero and villain, even down to clothing and makeup. The hero usually wore white or light colors, and was always natural, rustic, he-man or boy-next-door looking. The villain usually wore black and was rather sleek and foreboding, complete with patent leather hair and moustache.

The public was accustomed to leading men who were either debonair or dashing (Cary Grant, Fred Astaire), warmhearted and sincere (Gary Cooper, James Stewart), or conventionally courageous (Errol Flynn, Tyrone Power). The traditional hero has an unerring sense of right and wrong, no inner conflicts and he courageously battles and defeats outside forces. Some actors (Gable, Tracy, Paul Muni, James Cagney) played both traditional heroes and leading men with non-hero overtones with great success.

In the early thirties, Cagney especially played tough and villainous characters with sympathetic overtones, but there was never any doubt that since they were basically "undesirable" characters, good would triumph and they would receive their "just deserts."

Garfield began a new trend in which qualities of good and evil were not so clearly drawn; he was a complex individual who felt society had wronged him; there was a glimmer of hope for his reformation, but not a guarantee. He was the first hero (leading man) who fought forces from both within and without.

The rebel hero is seldom a man of action. He has "dropped out" of society in one way or another and lets others be activists, although he is often a catalyst. He is a sensitive, often inarticulate character. He is usually filled with pathos and although sometimes uncommunicative he embodies in his personality not only sensitivity but virility and innate intelligence.

The screen rebel usually lacks ambition, is a loner set apart from his companions, but has a streak of nobility, a great deal of personal pride, idealism and individuality. He possesses Hamlet-like qualities and through his rebellion he often discovers his own insufficiencies, human failings, and corruptibility. He rebels against society but makes little attempt to change it. He seldom, if ever, rises above his problems.

Anti-heroes (or non-heroes) are also loners. They are cynical men with no idealism at all but they have a strong personal code. *They* do not "drop out" but endure and conquer in a corrupt society. Both the traditional hero and anti-hero fight only outside forces and always overcome their problems. Like the character Bogart introduced in *Dark Victory* then later played to perfection in *The Maltese Falcon* and *Casablanca*, and the characters Dick Powell and Robert Montgomery portrayed in their postwar detective films, anti-heroes are sophisticated, know both sides of the law but are tough enough to win out while they maintain their

personal code and are still romantic enough to get the girl. Gable epitomized the combination of traditional hero and anti-hero in *Gone With the Wind*.

The anti-hero in films did not truly emerge until *The Maltese Falcon* in 1941. The anti-hero gained popularity in the 1940s and 1950s, probably due to the cynicism during and following World War II. People were relating to the hip non-hero who was not involved in world problems but devoting his time to overcoming his own personal problems.

The rebel heroes in this book are actors who have portrayed rebel personalities on screen and who themselves possess qualities which enable them to project these characterizations successfully. They are often rebels in their personal lives.

In almost every case, these actors have gained immediate popularity with movie audiences, especially youth and women. Women in particular react to their sultry animalism and rare combination of sensitivity and toughness. They appeal to the young because they represent the search for value and meaning in a materialistic and adult-oriented society, while still retaining a certain amount of idealism.

Movies such as *Dead End* (1937) realistically depicted urban life and prepared audiences for the emergence of the screen rebel. Millions of people across the land empathized with the oppressed, lost, uncommunicative malcontent that Garfield introduced in *Four Daughters* (1938). They saw in him, as did the character portrayed by girl-next-door co-star Priscilla Lane, underlying characteristics of goodness and sensitivity. She, along with all the women in the audience, felt that love could reform him.

Garfield played the same role with slight variation for the next thirteen years. The rebel image was continued

John Garfield, the screen's first rebel hero.

in the late forties and early fifties by Montgomery Clift and Marlon Brando. (Even Frank Sinatra played rebel heroes in several of his films, adding the facet of hip sophistication to the character.) James Dean carried it further, playing even more uncommunicative and troubled characters. Paul Newman, Steve McQueen and Warren Beatty emphasized the underlying current of sexuality inherent in the rebel.

English contributions include Albert Finney, Richard Harris, Michael Caine and David Hemmings, rebelling against the mores of the British Establishment.

Most recently, with the emergence of a more affluent society, a move to suburbia, and the widespread use and acceptance of drugs, young people have found rebel heroes in Dustin Hoffman and Peter Fonda.

Thus, though the basic type remains the same, the rebel hero of the screen has run the gamut in the last thirty years from the John Garfield character—reared in poverty and rising from the slums—to Dustin Hoffman in *The Graduate*, rebelling against the meaninglessness of his middle-class affluence, and Peter Fonda in *Easy Rider*, rebelling against conformity through the use of drugs.

This book will be primarily concerned with the evolution of the rebel hero character. It is not intended as a biography of any of the stars who have played such roles. We will not discuss in depth the careers of these people outside of their rebel hero characterizations. The personal lives of the actors will be discussed only insofar as their off-screen rebellion influenced the public's acceptance of them as rebel heroes.

Through the years there have been many roles and many actors that have had characteristics of both rebel and anti-hero. Some actors, like Newman and McQueen, can successfully bounce between rebel hero and anti-hero parts. Many actors who portray rebels go on, like Brando, Newman and McQueen, to become super-stars by carrying their personal magnetism to non-rebel roles and winning acceptance from wider audiences. Others never escape type-casting.

Traditional heroes Cary Grant (with Mary Brian),
Tyrone Power (with Loretta Young) and James Stewart.

Clark Gable combined traditional hero and anti-hero qualities as Rhett Butler in *Gone With the Wind*.

Humphrey Bogart, perhaps the first true anti-hero of the screen. His characters always did the right thing, even if for the wrong reason.

Spencer Tracy and Clark Gable, pictured here in *Boom Town*. They were two of the actors who were able to successfully portray traditional heroes with non-hero overtones.

Joel McCrea, Humphrey Bogart and Allen Jenkins in *Dead End* (right), a film which paved the way for John Garfield's appearance as the screen's first rebel hero in *Four Daughters* (pictured above with Priscilla Lane).

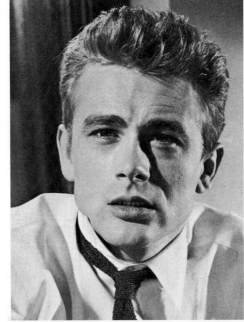

Garfield and some of the men who continued
to carry the torch of the rebel hero.

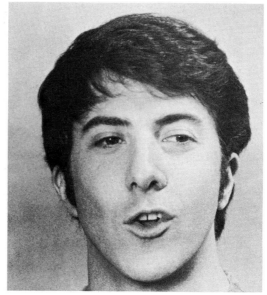

9

1
The Rebel Hero:
Launched and Almost Lost

By 1938, the country had undergone eight years of the Depression. Franklin D. Roosevelt was in his second term, and Americans had accepted the fact that times were hard and prosperity a long way off. Preparations for war were going on in Europe and Asia. At home, the government set up WPA camps and projects to keep youth busy and off the unemployment rolls.

Art as always reflected the times, and novelists, poets and playwrights wrote of America's oppressed and wandering people. John Steinbeck's *The Grapes of Wrath* best captured the problems of rural Americans out of work and migrating to other areas of the country to eke

out a survival. Plays such as *Street Scene* and *Dead End* depicted the plight of urban Americans already trapped in ghetto and slum conditions and now reacting to further economic hardships, often turning to crime.

Bonnie Parker and Clyde Barrow had started as small-time bank robbers in the Southwest in the 1930s. Within a few years they were on FBI lists of "Most Wanted Criminals." Ironically, Bonnie and Clyde, like many of the other "most wanted," became folk heroes to the socially and economically depressed population of the day. People simultaneously feared and admired the desperadoes for breaking out of a hopeless existence.

Although many books and plays were concerned with the economic conditions of the day, films in the 1930s generally avoided the subject.

Most of the motion picture companies were grinding out escapist fare, on the theory that the public was interested only in pure entertainment—"If you want to send a message, call Western Union" was the credo.

Paramount turned out comedies about the super-rich, with a few De Mille spectacles and Mae West vehicles thrown in. Metro concentrated on shopgirl soap operas led by Joan Crawford (usually portraying a salesgirl dressed in gowns by Adrian), romantic dramas starring Greta Garbo and Norma Shearer, action-adventures with Clark Gable and Spencer Tracy. The Marx Brothers did comedies for both studios.

Universal and Columbia produced mostly "B" films, Westerns, horror films, and occasional musicals and comedies. They did not have the stable of stars the other studios had, and relied on loanouts and free-lancers.

Deanna Durbin's escapist films are credited with saving Universal in the mid-1930s. Another child star, Shirley Temple, was instrumental in keeping 20th Century-Fox in the black. Sonja Henie, Alice Faye, and Tyrone Power also brightened the pictures at Fox. RKO relied on Fred Astaire and Ginger Rogers, dancing and singing their way through a white tie-and-tails world that existed only on sound stages. Monogram, Republic and Grand National produced Westerns and action-adventures.

The "B" film, initially "pushed" on exhibitors if they wanted "A" films, had become such a staple in the movie heyday of the thirties that the situation was reversed—by 1938, "B" films were used as leverage to sell some "A" films.

Although United Artists released such memorable films as *Street Scene* (1931), *Arrowsmith* (1932), *Les Miserables* (1935), and *Dead End* (1937), only one of the major studios—Warner Bros.—seemed to have a social consciousness during the thirties. Warners was often described as the studio that produced films for and about the working class, with directors such as Michael Curtiz and Mervyn LeRoy.

Along with its gangster adventures and musical extravaganzas, the studio managed to produce some memorable biographical films (*The Story of Louis Pasteur, The Life of Emile Zola*), and some socially significant ones (*I Am a Fugitive From a Chain Gang, Green Pastures, Black Legion, They Won't Forget*). In the thirties, it was Warner Bros. that tackled controversial themes, and the controversial themes of the day dealt with the Depression. Looking back, many now interpret the films as somewhat socialist-oriented. It was Warners who signed the Dead End Kids, and it was to be expected that it

Thirties movies were generally escapist fare. Boxoffice stars included Shirley Temple, Deanna Durbin, Joan Crawford (with Robert Montgomery), Ginger Rogers and Fred Astaire.

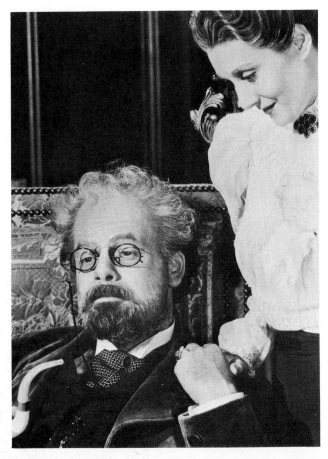

Warners was the most socially conscious studio.
During the thirties they produced memorable biographies,
such as *The Life of Emile Zola* with Paul Muni.

John Garfield was a "startling innovation in screen characters"
in *Four Daughters*. (Here with Jeffrey Lynn.)

would be Warners who would sign John Garfield, an unconventional actor who epitomized the social unrest of the era.

It is difficult, over thirty years later, to realize the impact that John Garfield had on movie audiences of 1938. He was an entirely new kind of screen personality.

The Warner Bros. production of *Four Daughters* was a simple, charming story of a musical family in a small, average American town. Its rather corny plot revolved around the youngest daughter (Priscilla Lane) and her encounters with a typical suitor (Jeffrey Lynn) and an atypical suitor (Garfield). The film opened August 9, 1938, at Radio City Music Hall, and was an immediate success with the public and the critics.

"As the most startling innovation in the way of a screen character in years, a fascinating fatalist, reckless and poor and unhappy, who smokes too much, who is insufferably rude to everybody and who assumes as a matter of course that all the cards are stacked against him," *The New York Times* noted, "Mr. Garfield is such a sweet relief from conventional screen types."

In ads for *Four Daughters*, Jack Warner boasted that the film was·the climax of his career. Even the conservative *New York Times* conceded, "It's one of the best pictures of anybody's career, if only for the sake of the marvelously meaningful character of Mickey Borden as portrayed by John Garfield, who bites off his lines with a delivery so eloquent that we still aren't sure whether it is the dialogue or Mr. Garfield who is so bitterly brilliant."

Proving that it is a combination of both role and qualities of actor that creates this special hero, the *Times* continued: "Our vote, though, is for Mr. Garfield and for whatever stars watch over his career on the stage and screen, because, on rereading the dialogue, as we have just done carefully, it seems to have lost something of the acidity, the beautiful clarity it had when Mr. Garfield spoke it."

The film, based on a short story by Fanny Hurst, was written by Julius J. Epstein and Lenore Coffee. They described Mickey Borden: "His dress is careless, almost shabby. But he is fortunate that his carelessness adds to his attractiveness. His manner is indolent, his expression wry, almost surly. His humor is ironic. When he smiles (which is seldom), his demeanor is sardonic. Mickey Borden doesn't think well of himself or the world. Poverty had done the trick."

John Garfield's personal and professional background made him a natural for the part. He *was* Mickey Borden. One of the memorable scenes of the film shows him sitting at a piano (Borden is an out-of-work orchestrator) with a cigarette dangling from his lips. He explains to

Priscilla Lane that "they" are to blame for his misery. Garfield projected then what he would project in a dozen more films and what he was in real life—the eternal outsider.

This defeatist character, this moral weakling, was indeed an innovation for the screen. Some critics have called the Mickey Borden character socialist-oriented (American Communists, it has been said, found social significance in all Garfield films). Borden, like many subsequent Garfield characters, is an iconoclast, embittered and lashing out at every convention and institution sacred to the middle class. He is a laconic, urban, shiftless vagabond who upsets the life of a small town (hence, in the thirties, average) family.

This is Mickey's first encounter with kindness, sensitivity and genuine love, as offered by Priscilla Lane, though he shocks her and the audience, used to traditional heroes, with his iconoclastic attitudes.

The Priscilla Lane character in *Four Daughters* set the pattern for the rebel hero's heroine in many films to come. She has heroic integrity and a strength of character unlike most screen heroines, who can rely on traditional American heroes or hard-bitten anti-heroes. She is strong enough to maintain her own values as well as to aid her rebel hero in finding his own values.

In *Four Daughters*, Priscilla marries Mickey Borden and they endure life together for a while, but Borden's better self is honest enough and possesses enough courage to realize finally that he is no good for her and that he is beyond the reformation of which she dreams. Realistically, he causes his own death.

(Ironically, Warners re-made the film seventeen years later as *Young at Heart*, with Frank Sinatra and Doris Day, and tacked on an unrealistic Hollywood ending in which the suicide attempt failed and the characters were reunited.)

As well as being critically acclaimed, *Four Daughters* was a huge commercial success and John Garfield became an overnight star. As hackneyed as that phrase may be, it applied. Most "overnight stars" have been struggling for years. But *Four Daughters* was in fact Garfield's first film after a short, and though successful, not spectacular stage career.

In 1938, Garfield, the Dead End Kids, and Priscilla Lane headed Warner Bros.' list of featured players.

While the press agents touted that Garfield possessed a combination of talents reminiscent of James Cagney, Edward G. Robinson, and Spencer Tracy, Warner Bros., as was often the case under the old studio system, misused Garfield's talents and success in *Four Daughters* by casting him in a series of similar roles in inferior films. They also threw him into the Paul Muni-Bette Davis vehicle *Juarez*, in which he was the most out-of-place

Garfield, Priscilla Lane in *Four Daughters*.

The Four Daughters:
Rosemary Lane,
Gale Page,
Priscilla and Lola Lane.

and Bronx-accented Mexican revolutionary the screen ever produced.

Getting their money's worth, in 1939 Warner Bros. cast Garfield in five films. In addition to *Juarez*, he was starred in *Daughters Courageous* (a successor but not a sequel to *Four Daughters*), *They Made Me a Criminal*, *Blackwell's Island*, and *Dust Be My Destiny*.

They Made Me a Criminal was about a boxer wanted for murder who takes refuge on a farm. The love and affection of the people who live there reform him (of course, he is really innocent of the murder). The film was a remake of *The Life of Jimmy Dolan*, and co-starred the Dead End Kids. This group, headed by Leo Gorcey, Huntz Hall, and Billy Hallop, originated in the stage version of *Dead End*. They were brought to Hollywood by Sam Goldwyn to star in the film version. Gorcey was a sort of anti-hero gang leader of the group, and in most of their films Hallop served as a teenage Garfield-like quasi-rebel being corrupted by his environment, but not yet embittered.

The Dead End Kids (later the Bowery Boys) introduced juvenile delinquency to the screen. They too were immediately successful, but after a few "A" pictures, they were misused by Hollywood in the forties in a series of low-budget comedy-melodramas.

In *Blackwell's Island*, Garfield was a reporter who went to jail to expose prison corruption.

A little less than a year after *Four Daughters*, Warner Bros. released *Daughters Courageous*. Again, Michael Curtiz directed. The screenplay was by Julius J. and Phillip G. Epstein, and the official credits say it was "suggested by a play by Dorothy Bennett and Irving White."

Fanny Hurst, who wrote the original story on which *Four Daughters* was based, and Lenore Coffee, who collaborated on that screenplay with Julius Epstein, received no credit for *Daughters Courageous*, which seems absurd. It was obviously the same story, with slight variations—the four daughters were the same, but drama was their family interest instead of music and the setting was California instead of New England. There was one major difference—in this picture, John Garfield got star billing.

It was such an obvious attempt to capitalize on *Four Daughters* and Garfield's success in that film, that Archer Winsten in the *New York Post* noted, "*Daughters Courageous* is an undertaking so characteristic of a prevailing Hollywood practice that it deserves attention beyond the question of intrinsic merit. The quality of the script follows that trend of sequels . . . weakness of far-fetched situations and characters exploited beyond their normal limits. . . . Such a picture is made on the theory that you should strike while the iron (the public) is hot."

But Winsten and other reviewers still conceded that the film, not a sequel but a successor, had merits on its own.

John Garfield, Dead End Kids in *They Made Me a Criminal*. This was their only film together.

The Dead End Kids (here with Bogart) represented the Depression's displaced teenagers.

15

Billy Hallop in *Crime School*. Hallop had the charisma and all the qualities necessary for rebel hero stardom, but like the Dead End Kids, he was not allowed to develop his potential.

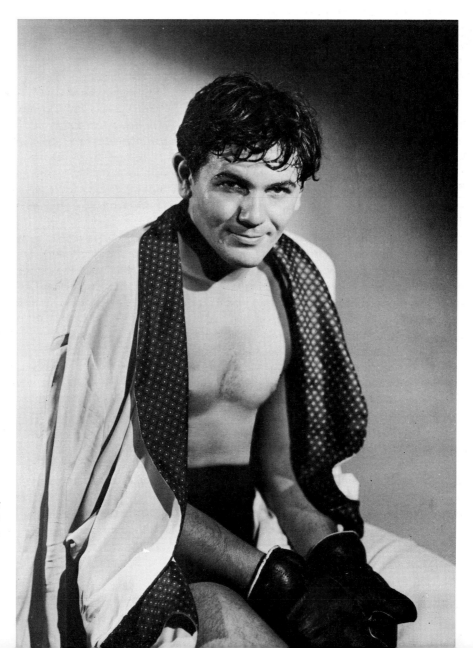

Garfield as the fighter
Jimmy Dolan in
They Made Me a Criminal.

16

Garfield, in this plot, as in *Four Daughters*, was a fatalistic, nonconforming interloper. This time he was the son of a no-account fisherman, and again Priscilla Lane had to choose between him and Jeffrey Lynn. Such Garfield lines as "To heck with work" and asking Priscilla Lane to "Buy me a beer" reinforced his rebel image. In this film, instead of killing Garfield off, the scripters had him walk off into the sunset to seek his fame and fortune, again leaving Priscilla with Jeffrey Lynn.

There seems to be no reason for having titled the film *Daughters Courageous*; perhaps Warners was trying to capitalize on the success of MGM's *Captains Courageous*.

To further cash in on the success of *Four Daughters*, in December 1939 Warners released a direct sequel, *Four Wives*, which starred the Lane Sisters, Claude Rains and Jeffrey Lynn. Michael Curtiz again directed and the film received excellent reviews. Garfield made a brief, unbilled appearance as the ghost of Mickey Borden.

In *Dust Be My Destiny*, the public and critics again found Garfield as an outcast absorbing the blows of a society that produced him.

"John Garfield, official gall-and-wormwood taster for the Warners, is sipping another bitter brew at the Strand in *Dust Be My Destiny*, latest of the Brothers' apparently interminable line of melodramas about the fate-dogged boys from the wrong side of the railroad tracks," wrote Frank Nugent in *The New York Times*. "Considering the practice they have had, it's not at all surprising that the picture goes its way smoothly, never missing a dramatic cue, a pause for laughter, a perfectly timed spurt of action when the utter futility of it all begins to grow too utterly utter. If that's the measure of success, the Warners can chalk up another. Personally, we're tired of the formula."

Nugent continued, "It's not even fun, anymore, outguessing the script. The moment we met Joe Bell riding a freight car, looking for work, we knew he was going to be sent to a prison camp. The moment we saw the prison gang foreman (whose step-daughter is Priscilla Lane) and heard about his whiskey heart, we knew Joe was going to be blamed for his death. The moment we saw Joe and Mabel getting married on a theatre's stage (for some furniture and a month's rent) we knew some one would take a picture that would bring the law on the run. The moment—but you know what happens as well as we do, right up to, and including the defense attorney's tear-drenched charge to the jury that 'if you convict this boy (quaver) you are convicting thousands like him, not criminals, not murderers, just nobodies trying to find a place to hang their hat.'

"Mr. Garfield, Miss Lane, Stanley Ridges as the prison foreman, Henry Armetta as proprietor of a diner, Alan Hale as a city editor and most of the others have played it well enough, although we detect signs in Mr. Garfield

Garfield, Paul Muni in *Juarez*. Totally miscast, Garfield was thrown into the film to cash in on his popularity.

of taking even his cynicism cynically, and of weariness in Miss Lane at having to redeem Mr. Garfield all over again."

"It's no career for an actress," Nugent concluded. "It shouldn't be a career for the Warners either but from what we've heard the end is not in sight. Between this picture and his next we're certain Mr. Garfield will have time to backslide. It's in his contract."

This was the first film in which Garfield was allowed to win the girl. But by this time, fans as well as critics were tiring of the formula role Warner Bros. was imposing on him.

Archer Winsten observed, "He is fate's whipping boy, a personification of the bloody but unbowed head, and the embittered voice of the dispossessed."

It is important to note that Garfield's on-screen personality (this applies to many ensuing screen rebels as well) was a direct extension of his off-screen self. Garfield's personal life reads like a plot from one of his early Warner Bros. vehicles. For in truth, John Garfield, born Julius Garfinkel on New York City's lower East Side on March 4, 1913, was the product of an environment which promised to make him bitter, oppressed, and possibly lead to a life of crime.

A poor boy whose father was a coat presser, Julius lost his mother when he was seven. His father remarried and took Julius to live with him in the Bronx. Julius's younger brother, Max, was left with an uncle in Brooklyn.

Julius began running with Bronx juvenile gangs, was expelled from several schools and became involved in petty thievery. He was saved from a life of crime by an

Italian-American child psychologist and educator, Dr. Angelo Patri. Patri improved Garfinkel's home conditions and put the boy in a drama class to correct his stutter. Julius had a natural aptitude for drama, and through Dr. Patri's influence he was given a scholarship in dramatics at the Heckscher Foundation Drama Workshop.

From this point on, his interest in acting was the mainstay of his existence. He kicked around for years, and in the early thirties became involved with Clifford Odets, a Bronx neighbor who recommended him for membership in the newly formed Group Theatre.

Garfield married his childhood sweetheart, Roberta Seidman, in the early thirties, and during the lean years she worked at office jobs while he gained acting experience in summer stock. He took a sales job at Macy's so they would have enough money to marry.

In February 1935, Garfield was featured in the Group Theatre production of Odets' *Awake and Sing* at the Belasco Theatre. He played the part of a young Bronx boy seeking the meaning of life. He received critical acclaim, and was made a full-fledged member of The Group. The *Variety* review predicted: "Jules Garfield looks headed for Hollywood."

The Group Theatre was simultaneously producing Odets' *Waiting for Lefty* at the Civic Repertory Theatre on 14th Street. That one-acter about taxi strikes was used by the Communists for agitation and propaganda purposes.

Garfield's next stage role was again with The Group, this time in their production of the antiwar musical, *Johnny Johnson*, by Paul Green and Kurt Weill. After that he left The Group, to join the road company of Elmer Rice's *Counsellor at Law*, which starred Otto Kruger. Garfield did so well in the road company, he was switched to the Broadway production which starred Paul Muni.

Daughters Courageous, a successor but not a sequel to *Four Daughters.*

This led to a part in the hit play, *Having a Wonderful Time.* It was the height of the Depression, and the average worker was making fifty cents an hour. Garfield's salary: $300 weekly. Julie Garfinkel, now Jules Garfield, twenty-four, had risen rapidly. Hollywood was eager to sign him, but he rejected all picture offers, saying he wasn't ready for Hollywood and didn't want to be bound by an exclusive contract. Besides, he was riding high. *Having a Wonderful Time* was set for a long run.

However, Garfield left the play when Odets practically guaranteed him the lead in The Group's upcoming production, *Golden Boy.* But Harold Clurman, the director, gave the lead to his brother-in-law, Luther Adler. In his book about the Group Theatre, Clurman said, "Garfield was obviously the type, but he had neither the pathos nor the variety, in my opinion, to sustain the role." Clurman cast Garfield in the comedy role of "Siggie," the boxer's cabdriver.

Embittered by the *Golden Boy* experience, and prodded by his wife Robbie, who probably had no desire to return to office work, Jules Garfield signed with Warner Bros. in 1938. They changed his name to John. The contract included a clause permitting him to do one play a year, after giving Warners sixty days' notice.

After *Four Daughters* was released, the Group Theatre offered Garfield the lead in the London production of *Golden Boy.* He refused it.

Apparently, Garfield was not—as many actors are—eager to make films. He said, "I came to Hollywood fully expecting to hate it and all set for the kick in the pants I felt sure I would get. In fact, when I signed with the studio I left a good, wide, neat and clean exit through which to make my farewell bow with as much grace as possible." He referred to the clause allowing him to do stage work. But over the next seven years, he exercised that clause only once.

Seemingly, he was also humble about his quick success. Discussing the part of Mickey Borden, he called it "foolproof and actor-proof" and his receiving it "pure, unadulterated luck and don't think for a minute that I ever kidded myself into thinking it anything else."

That same year, the Garfields had their first child, a girl. Despite initial disinterest in filmmaking, and although married and a father, Garfield quickly fell into the Hollywood social whirl. Over the next decade, gossip columnists linked his name with many Hollywood beauties, notably Hedy Lamarr.

19

Henry Armetta, Priscilla Lane, Garfield, Alan Hale in
Dust Be My Destiny. Garfield finally wins the girl.

Pat O'Brien, Ann Sheridan, John Garfield
Castle on the Hudson, a non-rebel role for Garfield.

The Garfields had a second child, David, in 1942.
(David has since changed his name to John Garfield, Jr.)
After his birth, the Garfields separated, but not legally.
In 1945, Garfield's daughter was suddenly taken ill after
a picnic and died a few hours later, probably the result
of a piece of food lodged in her windpipe. The girl's
unfortunate death briefly reconciled the Garfields, and
in 1946 they had another daughter, Julie.

After completing five films in 1939 and a routine
prison melodrama in 1940, *Castle on the Hudson*, (directed by Anatole Litvak and based on one of the stories
in *20,000 Years in Sing Sing*), Garfield returned to Broadway to portray the Overland Kid in *Heavenly Express*.
His co-stars were Burl Ives and Aline MacMahon. Critically, the play was only a moderate success.

If Garfield hoped his return to Broadway would jolt
Warner Bros. into ending their type-casting of him, he
miscalculated. No sooner was he back in Hollywood
when he was cast in *Saturday's Children* as another "sal-
low Romeo with a sad face and a troubled soul."

But *Saturday's Children* was a success. Howard Barnes
in the *New York Herald Tribune* said, "John Garfield,
who raised our hopes too high in his first screen acting,
justifies those hopes in this production. He plays with
the sensitive, thoughtful authority that he knows how to
muster, as the more or less beaten hero of the tale."

The Epstein brothers again wrote the screenplay,
based on Maxwell Anderson's play about the office
working class in New York City. Bosley Crowther in *The
New York Times* noted, "No studio in Hollywood seems

After a stint on Broadway, Garfield returned to films in
Saturday's Children, here with Roscoe Karns and Anne Shirley.

John Garfield, Frances Farmer, Pat O'Brien in *Flowing Gold*.
Oil pictures were "in" that season.

Garfield was a villain in *East of the River*.
Brenda Marshall was interested.

Hedy Lamarr and John Garfield in *Tortilla Flat*, one of Garfield's
two loan-outs to MGM, a studio he liked working for.

to have a more consistent regard for the middle class, with its myriad little sorrows and triumphs, its domestic delights and dissensions, than Warner Bros., whose latest compliment to the proud but hard-pressed poor is paid in *Saturday's Children*." Crowther also noted that Garfield "falls into the part of the harassed young lover as though it had been written for him alone."

Although he was type-cast, *Saturday's Children* was at least a first-rate script and allowed Garfield's screen character some development. But again he was thrown into a second-rate film in which the rebel character remained stagnant. *Flowing Gold* was a story of oil wildcatters, and Warner Bros. rushed its New York opening to beat out MGM's oil story, *Boom Town*. Garfield portrayed Johnny Blake, a hunted murderer (he killed in self-defense), a good worker but with a chip on his shoulder. The story was very similar to *They Made Me a Criminal*. The New York Times said, "Mr. Garfield is still Mr. Garfield, which is good enough to make one wish that his producers would cease casting him in the same role, film after film. In fact, we don't think Mr. Garfield was running away from a murder rap at all. He was just a fugitive from Warners."

The *New York Herald Tribune* agreed. "Mr. Garfield is fine, but his many performances as a cynic weaned on suspicion tend to become monotonous."

Garfield's next film, *East of the River*, was released a month later. Again he played a wastrel with a streak of nobility, and even the fan magazines were pleading for the studio to free Garfield from the one-dimensional characters he was forced to play.

The rebel hero character so brilliantly launched by Warner Bros. had not been put to good use. But with the coming of World War II, the Depression ended, and so did the public's interest in oppressed, embittered, non-activist characters like Mickey Borden. The country and the motion picture industry were on a wartime footing. People were interested in involvement. At the same time, the anti-hero had been born, and, in the person of Humphrey Bogart, was enjoying great success in films like *The Maltese Falcon*, *All Through the Night*, *Across the Pacific* and *Casablanca*. The public was reacting to a character who had enough guts to "do the right thing," even though he might be doing it for the wrong reason.

Garfield was established as a star, and the studio used him indiscriminately in a series of mostly forgettable films in the early forties—*Out of the Fog*, *Dangerously They Live*, *Tortilla Flat* (for MGM), *Air Force*, *Destination Tokyo*, *Between Two Worlds*, and the all-star revues *Thank Your Lucky Stars* and *Hollywood Canteen*.

Notable exceptions during this period were *The Sea Wolf* (1941) and *The Fallen Sparrow* (1943). In *The Sea Wolf*, he played the young outcast who defies the cruel captain, portrayed by Edward G. Robinson. This was not Garfield's film, however, since the key role belonged to Robinson. Alexander Knox, as the castaway novelist, Gene Lockhart as the drunken doctor and Barry Fitzgerald as the cook were outstanding.

Garfield, a Jack London enthusiast, was furious when Warners refused to lend him to Columbia for London's autobiographical *Adventures of Martin Eden* (1942) or to United Artists for *Jack London* (1943).

Garfield had an affinity for London and his work. Like Garfield, London had come from the working class and had become successful at an early age (twenty-four). He wrote what are considered rebel stories and essays about the working class and working class ideas and the heroic spirit of the common man. London was active in socialist movements, and found the transition from working class to wealth and success personally unfulfilling.

Warner Bros. did lend Garfield to RKO in 1943 for *The Fallen Sparrow*, a pro-Loyalist tale. Garfield had actively supported the Spanish Loyalists off-screen. This film is noteworthy because it gave Garfield the chance to play a role close to that of an anti-hero. It was a muddled melodrama of a tortured Spanish Loyalist who does not give the Nazis the information they want. They allow him to return to the United States and he is hunted—and haunted. He manages to triumph over both the Nazis and his own fears of insanity. Richard Wallace directed with such success that critics compared him to Hitchcock. "An intriguing and imaginative spy thriller, it foils the Gestapo without a super sleuth and it preaches an ideal without speechmaking," said the *New York Herald Tribune*. But by today's standards, the picture has little impact. It was not a commercial success.

Although Warners never made use of Garfield's full potential, they did star him in one other notable vehicle —*Pride of the Marines* (1945), for which he won his best notices since *Four Daughters*. This was the closest Garfield came to playing a traditional American hero. Based on the true story of Marine Sergeant Al Schmid, who was blinded by a grenade blast after killing two hundred Japanese at Guadalcanal, the film was done in semi-documentary style to show the months-long and fear-ridden struggle of a hero to recover his nerve to face the prospect of going through life blind. While a traditional hero in the sense that he was a courageous soldier, after his blindness the character possesses rebel hero traits. The pride mentioned in the title refers to the pride of an honest man in himself.

After his blindness, Schmid is filled with bitterness, fury, self-pity and despair. The film touches a bit on anti-semitism when a fellow Marine (a Jew) reminds Schmid that he has no monopoly on handicaps.

Eleanor Parker played Schmid's fiancée, a girl of strong

Robert Hutton, Bette Davis, John Garfield in *Hollywood Canteen*. In reality, Davis and Garfield *were* involved in running the USO Hollywood Canteen.

Garfield and George Tobias in *Air Force*, one of the programmers Garfield made for Warner Bros. during the war.

Edward G. Robinson, Garfield in *The Sea Wolf*.

The Sea Wolf was one of Garfield's better quality films during his Warner Bros. years.

"Pride" preceded *The Best Years of Our Lives* as a document of postwar rehabilitation.

Dane Clark, Anthony Caruso, John Garfield in *Pride of the Marines*.

spirit who convinces Garfield that she truly loves him, doesn't merely pity him. Garfield gave a brilliant portrayal of the cocky, self-reliant Schmid.

Scripter Albert Maltz, later to be one of Hollywood's "blacklisted" writers, was accused by some critics of the day of injecting too much "social consciousness" in the tale of Schmid's working class origin and early life.

Nevertheless, the film, released in August 1945, was a vastly pertinent post-war picture. Preceding *The Best Years of Our Lives*, a larger scale production (1946), it attempted to help returning veterans—especially the handicapped and their families—to adjust to postwar conditions.

George Tobias, Garfield, Walter Brennan in *Nobody Lives Forever*.

John Garfield, *Nobody Lives Forever*, another inferior script wasting Garfield's talents.

Time Magazine said the film was "More than a rostrum for liberal polemics. It is a good, hard-hitting movie." The film was produced by Jerry Wald and directed by Delmer Daves. Ironically, the ads picture Garfield, Parker and Dane Clark walking arm in arm smiling, as if in an MGM musical instead of a Warners' social drama.

During the war and the postwar period, a new type of screen hero was emerging. Alan Ladd, Robert Mitchum, Kirk Douglas, Burt Lancaster (and others) all projected strong personalities and might have been rebel heroes. But the time was not right for a new rebel, nor were the proper rebel roles being written. Thus Ladd, who first had impact in *This Gun For Hire* (1942) as a villain, made a quick transition to anti-hero in *The Glass Key* and *Lucky Jordan*. In the late forties, Kirk Douglas and Burt Lancaster played roles bordering between anti-hero traditional hero and almost-villain. Robert Mitchum began a career which allowed him to jump from distinct hero roles to distinct anti-hero roles, with an occasional villain role thrown in.

By the late forties, the public was accepting stars in a considerably wider range of roles. The hardbitten anti-hero character was being somewhat softened (Gable in *The Hucksters*) and the traditional American hero was more realistic (James Stewart in *It's a Wonderful Life*).

As of 1945, however, there was no new rebel hero on the horizon. It semed that with the blending of the traditional and anti-hero, the rebel character had been a stepping stone, now all but forgotten.

After *Pride of the Marines*, Warners lent Garfield to MGM for *The Postman Always Rings Twice*. He starred with Lana Turner in James Cain's story of uncontrolled passion culminating in murder.

He returned to Warners to finish his contract, and was thrown back into a pseudo-rebel gangster mold in the potboiler, *Nobody Lives Forever*. Garfield played a con man out to swindle Geraldine Fitzgerald. He falls in love with her, eventually pays off his partners, and "goes straight"—another "reformed-by-the-love-of-a-good-woman" plot.

His last film under the Warners contract was *Humoresque*, with Joan Crawford. This time Garfield played an intellectual young violinist from the Lower East Side hoisted to prominence by wealthy patroness Crawford, who falls in love with him. Not surprisingly, since Clifford Odets wrote the screenplay (with Zachary Gold, based on a Fanny Hurst story), The Garfield character had similar motivations to those of the violinist-boxer of *Golden Boy*. In *Humoresque*, the psychological and materialistic drives of the violinist were stressed. Garfield was his most iconoclastic and obnoxious self since *Four Daughters*. ("Bad manners . . . an infallible sign of talent," observed Crawford.) The film received mediocre

reviews but was a commercial hit. "A remarkable variation of the Svengali theme," said Howard Barnes.

Free of his Warners contract, Garfield starred in a
revival in Hollywood of *Awake and Sing*, produced by
the Laboratory Theatre.

He formed his own production company, Enterprise
Studios. Wisely, he had no intention of suddenly changing his screen image. On the contrary, he knew what
he could do best. His first independent production was
Body and Soul, directed by Robert Rossen from a script
by Abraham Polonsky. This was the best picture of Garfield's career, and he received his one and only "Best
Actor" Oscar nomination.

In *Body and Soul*, Garfield was a boxer who sacrificed
honor, family and friends for fame and money. The
emphasis was on the Depression—"It was a long, hard
climb . . . rotten and hard and tough," the fighter tells
his girl. In this role, Garfield's rebel character as introduced in *Four Daughters* now becomes an activist. Again
it was the Depression, only this time he was in the slum
environment that spawned him and not in Warner Brothers' version of middle-America. He fights "the forces" by
using his natural abilities as a boxer to push his way up
into society. And then he becomes a victim of the
society he wanted so desperately to conquer. Lili Palmer,
representing the "good girl," is kicked in the teeth by

The critics hailed and the public reacted to the chemistry between Lana Turner and John Garfield in
The Postman Always Rings Twice.

John Garfield in one of the realistic fight scenes from *Body and Soul*.

Oscar Levant, Garfield in *Humoresque*. Elements of *Golden Boy* were present.

Joan Crawford, John Garfield in *Humoresque*. Crawford was fresh from her *Mildred Pierce* triumph, Garfield from *The Postman Always Rings Twice*.

John Garfield, Lilli Palmer *Body and Soul*.

29

1944 photograph featuring Eleanor Roosevelt, Red Skelton, Lucille Ball, John Garfield at Mrs. Roosevelt's birthday party.

Garfield, David Niven, Lilli Palmer on the set of *Body and Soul*. Niven starred that year for Garfield's Enterprise Studios in *The Other Love*, opposite Barbara Stanwyck.

Garfield in favor of the momentary pleasures of trampy Hazel Brooks. Thus the heroic "good woman" is realistically thrust aside, since Garfield's character is beyond reformation.

Critic Otis Guernsey in the *New York Herald Tribune* said: "He gives it a brooding authenticity as he pounds his way to the championship, becoming less and less scrupulous and more and more apt to lose his quick flashing temper on his friends. His is a growing characterization. He advances from arrogant youthful enthusiasm to the disillusioned competence of a 35-year-old champ with perfect ease and logic."

Time said: "John Garfield, having dropped some of his Dead End mannerisms, gives a good performance that is as hard and simple as a rock." They added, "A good deal of the picture has the cruelly redolent illusion of reality that distinguished many of the movies of low life made early in the thirties."

Black actor Canada Lee garnered great reviews for his performance as a doomed over-the-hill boxer.

At the time of release, *Body and Soul*, along with receiving rave reviews, was a very topical film because of New York State investigations into the "fixing" of sports events, notably boxing. The film was hailed for its great ring photography (James Wong Howe won the Oscar for Best Cinematography) and its realistic handling of what could have been a run-of-the-mill prizefight yarn.

Polonsky has said that it was a fight to keep director Rossen from rewriting the script. At the end of the picture, the boxer regains some semblance of dignity and nobility by defying "the mob"—as well as losing all he owns (he had bet on himself to lose)—by winning the fight in which he is supposed to take a dive. When confronted by the revengeful mobsters and his implied fate, he asks, "What can you do, kill me? Everybody dies." (Rossen also shot his own less effective ending, showing the fighter killed, ending up with his head in a garbage can.)

The fighter was a character much like John Garfield himself. His success had unsettled him, and he was searching for values he knew existed but couldn't define. Garfield's marriage had been shaky for years, and his friends and professional associates would soon lead him into trouble with the United States government. The government would accuse him of associating with known Communists, using his prestige as an actor to advance Communist causes, and making financial contributions to Communist front organizations and associations.

But in 1947, scandal was still four years away, and *Body and Soul* brought Garfield to the apex of his career. It was a personal as well as professional triumph, since it was his first independent production. Archer Winsten noted, "It's a striking commentary on Hollywood and its waste of talent that Garfield, an actor who was perfectly capable of doing his job nine years ago when he first left the New York stage, should have had to wait so long and impersonate so many ruinously repetitious types before he could realize his full capabilities."

Tommy Dorsey and John Garfield at a 1947 radio broadcast.

John Garfield, Jack L. Warner and Joy Page at the Hollywood premiere of *This Is the Army.*

Former "Our Gang" child star Jean Darling, with John Garfield and Sheila Rogers, eating with the troops in Italy during World War II.

2
New Rebel Hero Stars Emerge

After the success of *Body and Soul* in 1947, John Garfield made a brief (twenty-minute) appearance for Fox in *Gentleman's Agreement,* directed by Elia Kazan.

If Warners was the studio most socially conscious in the 1930s, it was Fox that picked up the socially significant themes in the 1940s. They produced *The Grapes of Wrath* in 1940, *The Ox-Bow Incident* in 1943, and in the late forties, films such as *The Snake Pit* and *Pinky.*

Gentleman's Agreement was one of several films after World War II to deal with antisemitism. Garfield received star billing under Gregory Peck and Dorothy McGuire for his featured role as the Jewish friend of a

writer (Peck), who is posing as a Jew to write a series of magazine articles on antisemitism.

Garfield told a friend, "That was a part I didn't act. I felt it with all my heart." *Gentleman's Agreement* won the Academy Award and New York Film Critics Award as Best Picture, and Kazan won the Oscar for Best Director.

In 1948, when his name was being linked to Communist front organizations, Garfield returned to New York to star on Broadway in ANTA's production, *Skipper Next to God* by Jan de Hartog. That year Garfield had refused the lead in *A Streetcar Named Desire,* claiming that the part of Blanche overshadowed that of Stanley

Henry Fonda in *The Grapes of Wrath*.

Jeanne Crain, Ethel Barrymore in *Pinky*.
In the forties, Fox had taken the torch
from Warners as the studio producing
socially significant dramas.

Minna Gombell, Olivia de Havilland,
Leo Genn, Mark Stevens *The Snake Pit*.

Kowalski. The part went to a then little-known actor,
Marlon Brando, who had played Nels in the stage version of *I Remember Mama* and had a brief personal
success in a flop play, *Truckline Café*.

Garfield won the Antoinette Perry Award for his performance in *Skipper Next to God*. "I wanted to do 'Skipper' because it is the story of a man and his conscience.
A story of a man who has to make decisions," Garfield said.

33

Before Garfield's next film, *Force of Evil*, was released late in 1948, movie audiences were introduced to Montgomery Clift. Another young actor recruited from the Broadway stage, Clift came to Hollywood in 1947. He would be the first of a dozen young men who would take the rebel hero torch from Garfield, add some new insights, and develop the character for the next twenty years.

Stubborn individualism in a sensitive male endeavoring to surmount harsh realities was epitomized by Clift's version of the screen rebel. Unlike the characters played by Garfield and later Brando, Montgomery Clift gave the impression of being uncommunicative not because he was uneducated or inarticulate but because he was aloof, assured and quietly determined to endure and overcome.

Clift had been wooed by Hollywood since the early forties. He had been a child star with Alfred Lunt and Lynn Fontanne in the production of *There Shall Be No Night*. Another of his stage successes was as the son in Thornton Wilder's *The Skin of Our Teeth*. When Clift, gazing down into the orchestra pit where Tallulah Bankhead had disappeared into a tent with an amorous lifeguard, delivered the line: "Mama, he knows her *real* well," he brought the house down. The line, when read by subsequent actors, never had the same comic effect, because Clift projected his own brand of innocence. It was this quality of innocence—combined with Clift's traditional good looks—that Hollywood wanted.

After "Skin," Clift played the disillusioned and embittered young casualty in Lillian Hellman's anti-appeasement play, *The Searching Wind*. He was a young veteran crippled in the war who wanted to know why the principles he fought for were still not realities.

Clift refused Hollywood offers for the next three years, until after the failure of *You Touched Me*, the Broadway play by Tennessee Williams and Donald Wyndham, based on a D. H. Lawrence story. Reportedly Clift was $1300 in debt and collecting unemployment insurance when Howard Hawks signed him to star with John Wayne in *Red River*, a psychological Western. It was Clift's first film. However *The Search*, his second film, was released first, in March 1948.

Postwar audiences were ready for a new hero, but not a conventional one. There was a communications gap— not between generations, but because values had changed. Hollywood discovered that pure escapist entertainment was no longer drawing people into theatres. The theme of most serious plays and movies during these postwar years centered on the difficulties human beings found in reaching out, finding, comforting, and communicating with one another.

A marked concern about reality began to manifest itself. In line with this, film acting became better because a certain sensitivity and depth was added to chacterizations. All this crystallized with Montgomery Clift. Up to this time, Hollywood had been dominated by personality actors. Even Garfield took over the screen much more by the force of his personality than by the depth of his acting.

The Search, directed by Fred Zinnemann, also had Jarmilla Novotna, the Metropolitan Opera soprano, Wendell Corey and Aline McMahon. A talented youngster, Ivan Jandl, played a small displaced boy who had become a derelict, almost wild animal in postwar Europe. The film was done in semi-documentary style and explored the relationship between an American GI (Clift) and the child.

Clift, through his sensitivity and understanding, tames the boy, teaches him English and brings him back into the fold of humanity. The child is eventually reunited with his mother. *Time* said: "*The Search* is the kind of picture which Hollywood should be thanked for sponsoring."

Postwar audiences found an immediate rapport with Clift's projection of wistful disillusionment. He became a new hero—deeply human, vulnerable, trying to do the right thing, but living in an arbitrary world. His performance in *The Search* won him an Academy Award nomination as Best Actor.

Red River was released a few months later. Human conflict was added to this story of cattle ranchers forced to drive their herds north to railroad connections. John Wayne portrayed a pigheaded frontiersman. Clift, as his foster son, opposed him in an excellent performance as a calm youth who rebels against Wayne's domineering ways and sides with the browbeaten herdsmen. By opposing Wayne's dictatorial policies, he gains Wayne's admiration and respect. Otis Guernsey in the *New York Herald Tribune* said: "Wayne plays what can best be described as a typical John Wayne role—tall, wooden and brute stubborn. Clift is much more interesting as a lean, dangerous, capable young man and he demonstrates that he can saunter into a Western with the best of them."

"*Red River* is not only a fulfillment for director Hawks," claimed *Time*, "It is a high promise for Montgomery Clift, who plays the thorny young man with a fresh blend of toughness and charm. [Note the similarity to early reviews of Garfield's screen personality.] He is that rare bird with both screen personality and acting talent."

The plot of *Red River* was not unlike the plot of *Mutiny on the Bounty*. The psychological conflict between two strong-willed men is the principal theme.

Wayne up to this point had been a traditional hero. Influenced by screenwriter Borden Chase, Wayne took this role of the semi-heavy, a Texas Captain Bligh, and Clift was the Western Mr. Christian. Wayne was happy

that the film was a huge success and that his new image could be utilized in subsequent movies. But it was hard for him to understand how a healthy America could love his bully character and still find Clift's character sympathetic. Could America love the guy who loses the fist fight?

Postwar audiences could. Whereas films during World War II had distinct enemies with distinct heroes battling them, the postwar generation found its enemies were not so clearly defined. Idealism was dying. People accepted the world as it was and identified with those who survived, by whatever means. They realized there were no answers—just questions. Since he could save no one else, each man sought values to salvage his own soul.

In *The Search* and *Red River*, Clift conveyed a sense of loneliness. He dealt with reality on the screen in such

Dorothy McGuire, Gregory Peck, John Garfield in *Gentleman's Agreement.* Garfield accepted the small role because it was a part "I felt I had to do."

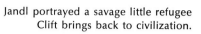
Jandl portrayed a savage little refugee
Clift brings back to civilization.

Aline McMahon, Ivan Jandl, Montgomery Clift in *The Search*.
Clift's sensitivity heralded a new kind of postwar hero.

Clift, Ivan Jandl in *The Search*.

Clift in *Red River*. It was *Mutiny on the Bounty* on horseback.

John Ireland, Montgomery Clift in *Red River*.

a way that film audiences sensed for the first time that isolation existed in the soul of man. Clift, like Garfield, was the "eternal outsider."

Unlike Garfield, who had risen from the slums, Clift's origin was one of relative wealth and security. He was born Edward Montgomery Clift on October 17, 1920, in Omaha to Mr. and Mrs. William Brooks Clift. He had a twin sister, Roberta, and an older brother, William Jr. The family moved quite often and took frequent trips to Europe.

After Clift's father lost his money in 1933, the family moved to Sarasota, Florida, and Montgomery got a part with an amateur theatrical company. In the summer of 1934, after they had moved to Connecticut, Mr. Clift got his son a part in *Fly Away Home* in the summer theatre at Stockbridge, Massachusetts. Thomas Mitchell was the star and director of that producion. The play was good enough for Broadway, and opened in January 1935 at the 48th Street Theatre. Mitchell again directed and starred, and Clift repeated his role. From this point on, Clift made his own decisions and arrangements about his career. His relationship with his family was never publicized.

A series of stage successes followed. *Dame Nature*, which didn't have a long run, provided him with a leading role as a shy, sensitive schoolboy who impregnates a lonely orphan. One of his friends discussing visiting Clift backstage at *Dame Nature* remembered "his hypersensitive quickness to misinterpret and mistrust, even at that age, before his personal furies set out in full pursuit of him."

Discussing the play, Richard Watts, Jr., then reviewing for the *New York Herald Tribune,* said: "Young Mr. Clift has an enormously difficult characterization to manage and on the whole handles it excellently, although there are times when he makes the youthful father too neurotic for comfort."

This neurotic acting style may have been the reason Clift was dismissed from *Life With Father* after only five performances (he had played Clarence Day, Jr.). But he lost no time obtaining another role, that of the young son in *There Shall Be No Night.* Alfred Lunt and Lynn Fontanne were the stars, and the play ran for two years, during which time Clift and the Lunts became inseparable. Many have said that Clift's acting style, though unique, was influenced by Lunt.

Like Garfield, Clift was a product of the New York stage. But unlike Garfield, once Clift was established as a movie star, he didn't return to the stage until his film career was waning. Although a Hollywood holdout initially, once there Clift enjoyed playing the role of Movie Star. By the end of 1948, after *The Search* and *Red River* had been released, Clift was established as a major star. He was on the cover of *Life. Look* presented him with its Achievement Award and named him "The Most Promising Star on the Hollywood Horizon."

Although a producer threatened to have Clift blackballed when he refused to sign a long-term contract after a screen test (prior to *Red River*), Clift still remained fiercely independent and demanded script approval and no long-term tie-ups.

He signed a three-picture deal with Paramount which gave him the right of script approval, director approval and the option to appear in films for other studios and on the legitimate stage. It was an extraordinary contract for any star in the late forties, especially a newcomer.

Although Clift had introduced the elements which he would later use to play one of the definitive screen rebels (Prewitt in *From Here to Eternity*), in 1948 the rebel hero character still belonged to John Garfield. Garfield's only film that year was *Force of Evil*, released in December.

This was the second of Garfield's three independently produced films, and was released by MGM. The other two were released by United Artists. Of all the Garfield films, *Force of Evil* is the only one with an *auteur* following. This is not because of Garfield, but because of screenwriter-director Abraham Polonsky.

Polonsky had written the screenplay for *Body and Soul,* and he collaborated on the screenplay for *Force of Evil* with novelist Ira Wolfert, who wrote the novel *Tucker's People,* on which the film was based. Although Polonsky's direction won excellent reviews ("New to the business of directing, Mr. Polonsky here establishes himself as a man of imagination and unquestioned craftsmanship," said *The New York Times*), *Force of Evil* was a commercial flop. But that was not the reason Polonsky did not direct another film for twenty-one years. (In 1969, he wrote and directed *Tell Them Willie Boy Is Here* for Universal.) After *Force of Evil,* Polonsky wrote the screenplay for *I Can Get It For You Wholesale* (Fox) and later had a deal pending with 20th Century-Fox to write and direct a film. But Polonsky was blacklisted before his directorial career could get off the ground.

In some respects, John Garfield was playing a rebel character in *Force of Evil*. As in *Body and Soul,* the hero in *Evil* becomes involved with forces of corruption and eventually rebels against them and tries to redeem himself.

Force of Evil is about a lawyer (Garfield) who joins the numbers racket. He is not, like the fighter in *Body and Soul,* a product of a slum environment. He willingly and knowingly involves himself with gangsters for financial gain, whereas the fighter in *Body and Soul* became involved through circumstance. In *Force of Evil,* his small-time gambler brother, portrayed by Thomas Gomez, is killed by Garfield's gangster boss, Tucker. Although misinterpreted at the time as a typical gangster film, *Force of Evil* is basically the story of the disintegration of a man under the heavy burden of a sense of guilt or wrong.

Once again, there is the "honest girl," this time portrayed by screen newcomer Beatrice Pearson. Again, we find a heroic heroine who tries to lead the hero onto the right path. It is not Garfield's involvement with the girl, however, but the slaying of his brother which triggers his conscience and makes him do the "right thing." The film ends as he is about to give himself up to the police and expose Tucker. "I decided to help," he says. As in the end of *Body and Soul,* the character has summoned his last bit of self-respect to regenerate himself morally. (But years later, Polonsky stated, "the hero is about to confess to the police because that is the way we could get a seal.")

In 1949 Garfield portrayed an actual rebel—not a rebel hero—in Columbia's *We Were Strangers*. It was directed by John Huston and co-starred Jennifer Jones.

It was Clift's only Western.

Montgomery Clift and John Wayne
in the famous fight scene from *Red River*.

Joanne Dru, Clift in *Red River*. Like the native girl in
Mutiny on the Bounty, her role was not necessary to the plot.

Garfield played one of a band of revolutionaries in Cuba in the early thirties, determined to assassinate an important, corrupt family. Jennifer, as China Valdez, Cuban patriot, was Garfield's love interest.

That same year Nicholas Ray (who would later direct one of the definitive films on the rebel character, *Rebel Without a Cause*), did *Knock on Any Door*, starring Humphrey Bogart and John Derek. It was Bogart's first independent production and Derek's first film. Derek's character was 1949's version of the Dead End Kids. He represented juvenile delinquency and the cause of it—environment, not heredity.

Garfield returned to Broadway while the heat of the House Committee on Un-American Activities was reaching the shores of the sunny Pacific. In Odets' new play, *The Big Knife*, he portrayed Charlie Castle, a Hollywood star controlled by a ruthless studio head. (Castle had killed a child in a hit-and-run accident and was being blackmailed by the mogul into signing a new long-term contract.) It was a malicious exposé of Hollywood which Hollywood bought anyway. The film version, released in 1955, starred Jack Palance as Charlie Castle and Rod Steiger as the mogul.

New star Montgomery Clift made only one film in 1949, *The Heiress*. Clift played a fortune hunter zeroing in on a plain-Jane old maid (Olivia de Havilland) in New York in the 1850s. De Havilland won her second Academy Award for this film, and although her performance was fine, one tends to think Academy members were

rewarding her for her performance in *The Snake Pit* a year earlier.

Clift's quality of innocence was used effectively by director William Wyler to set the audience up for the shock of discovering that this sincere, guileless character was indeed a coldblooded fortune-hunter as de Havilland's father had predicted.

The Heiress was a critical success but a box-office flop. Paramount used the profits from Cecil B. DeMille's overwhelming success, *Samson and Delilah*, to offset the losses on this film.

Some claim that Clift seemed totally unaware of the mores of the film's time. And Clift himself was not adjusting to the Hollywood of his own time. Violently independent, he backed out of Billy Wilder's *Sunset Boulevard* shortly before production was about to begin, and the part went to William Holden. Clift also refused *The Girl on the Via Flamina*, later made by Kirk Douglas as *Act of Love*.

Thomas Gomez, John Garfield in *Force of Evil*, which has become an *auteur* favorite.

Clift did star in one film in 1950, 20th Century-Fox's *The Big Lift,* co-starring Paul Douglas. George Seaton directed. It was similar to *The Search,* only this time Clift and Douglas were concerned with the Berlin airlift.

That year Garfield returned to the screen in two films —*Under My Skin* and *The Breaking Point*. Both films were partially based on Ernest Hemingway stories. In *Under My Skin*, Garfield was a crooked jockey. The Hemingway story, "My Old Man," tells of a boy's idolatrous devotion to his obviously shady father who has to race horses in Europe because he's been banned from American tracks. In the Hemingway tale, the old man never reforms and the kid only gets a small hint of his father's crookedness. But in this film adaptation, the boy discovers his father's crookedness and cruelty early

in the story and the last half of the film concerns the jockey's trying to redeem himself in his son's eyes but meeting an accidental death in the Grand Prix. The picture fits more into Garfield's gangster characterizations *(East of the River, Nobody Lives Forever)* than it does into his rebel characterizations. But there is the element of a woman who has principles a little better than his, and there is the ending where he "goes straight."

Before the release of *The Breaking Point* late in 1950, a new screen rebel had a fantastic impact on screen audiences. Like Garfield and Clift, he was an immediate success in his first film. Marlon Brando's brand of rebel hit the screen exactly at the time Garfield's star was descending.

40

Garfield in *Force of Evil*.

Garfield and Sid Stone in Polonsky's *Force of Evil*.

Garfield, Jennifer Jones in *We Were Strangers.*
He portrayed a revolutionary.

The Men (United Artists) opened at Radio City Music Hall in May, 1950. It co-starred Brando with Academy Award-winner Teresa Wright.

Brando had been beseiged with movie offers since his success on Broadway in *A Streetcar Named Desire.* Producer Stanley Kramer lured him to Hollywood with the challenging Carl Foreman script for *The Men* and a guarantee that Fred Zinnemann would direct. Brando received $40,000 for the picture (a strong salary for 1949). More importantly, he signed no long-term contracts and worked as a free agent.

The character he portrayed in *The Men* was reminiscent of Garfield's character in *Pride of the Marines.* Brando was a paraplegic veteran who initially rebelled against all attempts at treatment. Again it was the story of an embittered, angry young man who had to be "loved" back into accepting the harsh reality of his fate. And again, as they had with Garfield, the public reacted instantly and favorably.

Radio City Music Hall was again the launching pad for a new screen rebel. Bosley Crowther called Brando's performance "trenchant and stinging." A myth exists that in Brando's first few films all he did was mumble and scratch his way through. Crowther described Brando in *The Men:* "His face, the whole rhythm of his body and especially the strange timbre of his voice, often broken and plaintive and boyish, are articulate in every way. Out of stiff and frozen silences he can lash into a passionate rage with the fearful and flailing frenzy of a taut cable suddenly cut. Or he can show the poignant tenderness of doctor with a child."

While the film was a semi-documentary about paraplegics at the Birmingham Veterans Administration Hos-

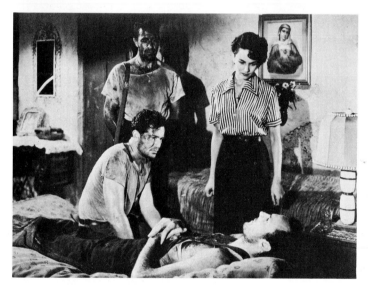

Gilbert Roland, Jennifer Jones, John Garfield in *We Were Strangers.*

pital near Hollywood, the plot revolved around the love affair between Brando, a sullen victim of the war unwilling to be rehabilitated, and his fiancée (Teresa Wright). She is the sweet, faithful girl who eventually convinces him that she loves-doesn't-pity-him. (Note the similarity to *Pride of the Marines.)* Again we have the reformation through the love of a good woman theme.

Time said the film was "notable for avoiding . . . the easy out. Its [the film's] basic theme is courage—courage in the face of utter hopelessness. It eloquently shows that cripples cannot get along with the world or themselves—and neither for that matter can normal people—unless they face reality and come to terms with it."

42

The subplots in the film concerned three other paraplegics—a well-educated cynic (Jack Webb), a horse-betting loafer (Richard Erdman), and a goodnatured Mexican-American (Arthur Jurado). The last was one of forty-five actual vets who acted in the film. Everett Sloane played a wise, conscientious doctor.

Most of the publicity about the picture concerned the fact that Brando lived for a month in the 32-bed ward at the hospital, observing the regimen of the paraplegics. *Newsweek* said, "Brando plays the crippled Wilozek with much the same sullen tenseness that made his Kowalski a memorable figure." Otis Guernsey said: "Every line he speaks carries meaning in the way he speaks it in a performance which depends not at all on personality but entirely on understanding of character and technical virtuosity." *Time* said, "Broadway's Marlon Brando . . . does a magnificent job. His halting, mumbled delivery, glowering silences and expert simulation of paraplegia do not suggest acting at all; they look chillingly like the real thing."

Not only did Brando and *The Men* receive critical acclaim and public acceptance but producer Stanley Kramer received a great deal of publicity about the fact that he attempted commercial films on controversial subjects. His two previous films were *Champion* and *Home of the Brave*.

"*The Men* ranks with the handful of extraordinary movies that do credit not only to their makers but to Hollywood," observed *Time*. "In an industry that lives by box office the film is remarkable, first of all for tackling a touchy subject: the salvage of war-wounded paraplegics, men hopelessly paralyzed from the waist down. More remarkable, the subject has been handled with frankness, taste and dramatic skill. . . ."

Fred Zinnemann, who had directed Montgomery Clift in his first film, directed Brando in *The Men*. But most of the acclaim for Zinnemann centered on his effective use of the paraplegics and capturing the aura of veteran hospital life.

Even before *The Men* opened, Brando's off-screen rebel image was notorious. People called him the first genuine character in Hollywood since Garbo. He refused to go along with the usual publicity measures. From the day Brando hit Hollywood he flaunted his individuality. They weren't going to make him give up his sweatshirt and bluejeans. Clothes-conscious Hollywood quickly dubbed him "The Slob." He shunned parties and Hollywood social life and alienated Hollywood's three top columnists, Hedda Hopper, Louella Parsons, and Sheilah Graham.

He especially alienated the Hollywood establishment because he was a proponent of the "Method," a naturalistic school of acting in which the actor is supposed to cease being himself and become the character.

Stories circulated around Hollywood concerning Brando's "serious approach to acting." While preparing for *The Men*, he learned to use a wheel chair and would roll himself around in public in order to get "the feel of the part." Several times, however, Brando caused consternation with this approach, because after accepting sympathetic words and looks, he would suddenly leap from the chair and shout, "I've been cured, I've been cured!"

These antics cast doubts on Brando's sincerity towards acting. Many thought his uniqueness was manufactured for publicity purposes. Nevertheless, *The Men* established him as a star. Whatever his critics disliked about him, they were unanimous in admitting that he was "an original." He defied easy comparison. No one was tempted to call him "the new Garfield," or the new anyone else. And from the beginning his talent surpassed Garfield in both range and depth.

Montgomery Clift, Olivia de Havilland in *The Heiress*. His innocence and good looks were put to good use.

Montgomery Clift in *The Big Lift*, a film he made for Fox while in Europe in 1950.

Clift and Paul Douglas in *The Big Lift*.

Jack Warner signed Brando to recreate his role of Stanley Kowalski in Elia Kazan's screen version of *A Streetcar Named Desire*, which would star Vivien Leigh. Brando's salary was a flat $75,000 on a one-picture, no-options deal.

John Garfield, who had inadvertently given Brando his big break by turning down the role of Kowalski, made his last good film in 1950. *The Breaking Point* was a Warner Bros. picture, produced by Jerry Wald and directed by Michael Curtiz. "I'm not the kind of actor that becomes a star in Hollywood," Garfield once stated. "I would normally have been a character actor but Mike Curtiz gave me the screen personality that carried me to stardom."

Curtiz, who launched and developed Garfield's screen image, obviously knew how to use him to best advantage. Although when viewed today *The Breaking Point* is to many extremely dated and sometimes laughable, in 1950 the film received rave reviews.

It was based on Ernest Hemingway's *To Have and Have Not*. Warners had made a film with that title in 1944 with Bogart and introducing Lauren Bacall, but the story had been completely changed and only the title remained. In 1947, Warners again used part of that story in another Bogart-Bacall film, *Key Largo*, directed by John Huston.

For *The Breaking Point*, writer Ranald MacDougall stayed very close to the character and story development as written by Hemingway. McDougall, did, however, change the locale from Florida to California, reshuffled incidents, and added some new characters. In the film Garfield played Harry Morgan, who has a wife, a couple of kids and operates a heavily mortgaged sports fishing cruiser. When a client leaves him stranded, he gets involved in a smuggling ring carrying Chinese laborers into the country. When that ends in disaster he gets involved in piloting a getaway boat for holdup men. *The New York Times* called the film "a four-base hit," and said "all of the character, color and cynicism of Mr. Hemingway's lean and hungry tale are wrapped up in this realistic picture and John Garfield is tops in the principal role."

Garfield himself said, "I think it's the best I've done since *Body and Soul*. Better than that."

Patricia Neal played the vamp, but it was Phyllis Thaxter, portraying Garfield's worn and jealous wife, who provided the film with an earthy credibility. Juano Hernandez played Garfield's ill-fated black mate and friend. The *Times* said, ". . . the suggestion of comradeship and trust that is achieved through the character . . . and the pathos created by his death, is not only a fine evidence of racial feeling, but is one of the most moving factors in the film."

A typical John Garfield tight spot in *Under My Skin*. The story was loosely based on Hemingway's *My Old Man*.

Like the leading character in *To Have and Have Not*, in this film Garfield was an anti-hero. He did not brood about his fate, but went out to try and make his way in the world even though he had "nothing to peddle but guts."

Time said, "The story is still tough, violent and essentially true to the book's central figure; a rugged individualist desperately down on his luck." *Time* also said: "In his meatiest role in years, actor Garfield gives one of his best performances. . . ."

It was unfortunate that Michael Curtiz could not have directed Garfield's upcoming appearance at a hearing of the House Committee on Un-American Activities.

The Committee had begun investigations of Communist infiltration into the motion picture industry in 1947. In 1951, after Garfield completed *He Ran All the Way*, but before it was released, he was called before the Committee.

Since 1947, various Hollywood elite, including L. B. Mayer, Jack Warner, and director Sam Wood, had gone before the House Committee and denounced certain writers and directors who were said to be members of

Garfield as the crooked jockey in *Under My Skin*.

46

the Communist Party. In December of that year, the studio heads got together and decided to blacklist the famous Hollywood Ten—writers and directors: Alvah Bessie, Herbert Biberman, Lester Cole, Edward Dmytryk, Ring Lardner, Jr., John Howard Lawson, Albert Maltz, Samuel Ornitz, Adrian Scott and Dalton Trumbo. Those people had refused to answer the Committee's questions at previous hearings, and had denied the Committee's right to interrogate them. The Communist Party created various "defense" agencies on their behalf. The "Committee for the First Amendment," among the founders of which were John Huston, William Wyler, and Phillip Dunne, circulated the *amicus curiae* brief on behalf of the Hollywood Ten, which Garfield signed. Only one of the Hollywood Ten subsequently confessed to having been a Communist and abjured Communism: Edward Dmytryk.

Various Hollywood luminaries and associates of Garfield such as Elia Kazan, Clifford Odets and Robert Rossen, confessed to having associations with the Communist Party, as did others, such as Budd Schulberg and Sterling Hayden.

Brando in *The Men*, his first film. Garfield was to be eclipsed.

The Red Scare had set in. In addition to the Hollywood Ten, many other actors, writers and directors were "unofficially" blacklisted, including Abraham Polonsky, Anne Revere, Gale Sondergaard and Michael Wilson. [Later, in 1954, a high court upheld blacklisting and threw out a suit against the studios by twenty-three actors and writers.]

Through the forties, Garfield had been an off-screen rebel in his politics. In a May 1947 issue of *Motion Picture* magazine, he advocated: "Actors should express their political convictions." Many of his films had had socialistic overtones and probably due to the environment which spawned him, Garfield was socialistic in his politcs, even though he was a wealthy and successful actor-producer.

When Garfeld initially testified early in 1951, he was accompanied by two of Hollywood's top lawyers, Louis Nizer and Sidney Davis. Garfield now denied beliefs he once professed and associations he once flaunted. His testimony before the Committee was so contradictory that journalists said he appeared moronic. When asked who persuaded him to sign the *amicus curiae* brief on behalf of the Hollywood Ten, he said: "Someone at the Beverly Hills Tennis Club." He couldn't remember if it had been a man or a woman.

Asked "Do you mean you would have just signed it if just anyone had walked up and asked you to?" He answered: "Not if it was any stranger."

Although he consistently denied knowing who it was, he ultimately said he thought it might have been George Willner. Willner was described by the Committee as a functionary in several well-known Communist enterprises.

Garfield denied he was a member of the National Council of the Arts, Sciences and Professions or had supported that organization, even though the Committee showed him a clipping from the Communist *Daily Worker* dated December 29, 1948, which referred to him as a signer of a statement urging the abolition of the Congressional Committee on Un-American Activities issued by the NCASP.

Garfield countered with statements that he hated Communism, considered it a tyranny that threatened the United States and the peace of the world. "I'm no Red, no Pink, no fellow traveller. I'd run like hell before lending my name knowingly to such a group." He said he was a "liberal Democrat" and thought the Communist Party should be outlawed and not allowed on the ballot "to protect Liberals like me."

The House Committee was not convinced. They called for an FBI investigation of Garfield. His Hollywood career came to an abrupt halt.

Garfield, Phyllis Thaxter in *The Breaking Point*.
It was closer to Hemingway's *To Have and Have Not*
than the Bogart–Bacall film with that title.

He Ran All the Way, produced by Garfield, was released in June 1951 through United Artists. The film, directed by John Berry and written by Hugo Berry and Guy Endore from a book by Sam Ross, told of a fugitive murderer terrorizing a middle class family he held hostage. Shelley Winters co-starred. The picture received poor reviews and was a commercial flop. It had a far-fetched plot and its poor reception was probably not due to Garfield's unfavorable publicity but because it was a bad film.

Unfortunately, *He Ran All the Way* was to be Garfield's last motion picture, a sad finale to a career which began brilliantly. Looking back on Garfield's thirty-one films, only three of four have aged well. His best is acknowledged to be *Body and Soul*, and many consider his next two best *Four Daughters* and its quasi-sequel, *Daughters Courageous*.

Two of 1951's critical and box-office blockbusters— *A Streetcar Named Desire* and *A Place in the Sun*— would firmly establish Brando and Clift as Hollywood's top male stars. The rebel hero of the screen was about to enter his golden age—and John Garfield, who started it all, would soon be the forgotten rebel.

Garfield, Juando Hernandez in *The Breaking Point*. Critics noted their rapport as fostering Negro–white brotherhood.

3
Clift and Brando

More than any other screen rebel, Marlon Brando epitomizes the rebel character off-screen. Hollywood has known "loners" and "characters," but Brando was the first male star to be a combination of the two.

From the moment he started to make films, Brando stated that motion pictures were, for him, a means to an end. He simply wanted to make enough money to lead the kind of life he envisioned as meaningful.

By Hollywood standards, he was in the big money immediately. After receiving $40,000 for *The Men* (1950) and $75,000 for *A Streetcar Named Desire* (1951), he received $100,000 for *Viva Zapata* (1952). Even by 1967,

long after his box-office drawing power was questionable, he reportedly received $750,000 per film.

Brando has never been known to live lavishly. In fact, in the early days, his father was his business manager and kept him on a small allowance. Brando invested his money shrewdly, and in the late fifties formed Pennebaker Productions (Pennebaker was his mother's maiden name) to produce films with and without Brando.

Brando's personal life has always been cloaked in mystery. He was born Marlon Brando, Jr., on April 3, 1924, in Omaha, Nebraska. His father, Marlon, Sr., had French forebears who spelled the name Brandeau. Brando has two older sisters—Frances, an artist, and Jocelyn, an actress. Jocelyn first used the professional name Hammer, but later changed it back to Brando.

Unlike Garfield and even Clift, there is no public information regarding Brando's early life that seems to psychologically warrant his rebellious attitudes. However, some reports say that there was conflict in his household because of his staid father's bourgeois businessman attitude vs. his mother's interest in the arts. This, however, seems far-fetched. It is a fact, though, that Brando was a discipline problem in school, but this was probably because he was an only son and a spoiled child.

His father, a manufacturer of chemical products and insecticides, was financially well off during the Depression. When Brando was six, the family moved to Evans-ton, Illinois, and then to Libertyville, both near Chicago. Brando (nicknamed Bud) left Libertyville High School to attend a private school in Minneapolis, the Shattuck Military Academy. Brando Sr. was not a disciplinarian, but the military academy could not discipline Bud either. He was expelled before graduation in 1943.

After he worked briefly in Libertyville digging ditches for a construction company, his father offered to finance a career in dramatics, and Marlon went to New York to live with his older sister Frances while he attended the Dramatic Workshop at the New School.

Brando always remained on the friendliest of terms with his immediate family. Whatever his childhood discipline problems, he always maintained strong family ties.

After several studio productions and summer stock, and after studying with Stella Adler and Elia Kazan,

Brando on the set of *The Men*.

Brando in *A Streetcar Named Desire*.

The demure Blanche (Vivien Leigh) has to endure the pig-like table manners of Stanley Kowalski.

Kim Hunter, Brando, Vivien Leigh.

Brando landed his first Broadway role in Kathryn Forbes' hit play, *I Remember Mama*, which opened on October 19, 1944.

In the Playbill for the show, Brando provided himself with an elaborate and highly fanciful biographical description. The Playbill said he was born in Calcutta, where his father was doing geological research. He was brought to the States when he was six months old.

In 1945, he didn't work at all. (Throughout his career Brando has often taken time off to travel and be by himself.) In April 1946, he returned to the stage. In *Truckline Café*, by Maxwell Anderson, he played Sage McRae, a war veteran who kills his faithless wife. It was an ill-fated play but its short run provided Brando with some good notices.

Guthrie McClintic saw Brando in *Truckline Café*, and gave him the role of Eugene Marchbanks in Katharine Cornell's revival of George Bernard Shaw's *Candida*. That year, Brando also played the role of a refugee Jew in Ben Hecht's play, *A Flag Is Born*, about the new country Israel, and later that same year he played the male lead opposite Tallulah Bankhead in *The Eagle Has Two Heads*. But Brando left the cast of the Jean Cocteau play before it reached New York and proceeded to spend about a year in study and foreign travel.

John Garfield's statement that the role of Blanche Du Bois would overshadow that of Stanley Kowalski in Tennessee Williams' *A Streetcar Named Desire*, seems absurd today. The most memorable aspect of Williams' hit play and subsequent movie was Brando's characterization of Kowalski. His torn T-shirt became a symbol of masculinity, and Brando's brooding, seething silences and bursts of mumbled dialogue established a new acting style.

The movie version of *Streetcar* was released in June, 1951. Vivien Leigh portrayed Blanche Du Bois and won her second Academy Award as Best Actress. Kim Hunter and Karl Malden, both recreating their stage roles, won Oscars as Best Supporting Actress and Actor. As Stanley Kowalski, the factory worker whose brute sensuality overwhelmed his already degraded alcoholic sister-in-law and drove her completely mad, Brando received his second consecutive Oscar nomination.

With this, only his second film, the name Marlon Brando became a household word and the cry "Stell-a" was heard throughout the land. Brando imitations were added to the repertoires of mimics and comedians.

Streetcar was a hit not only in America, but resulted in worldwide praise and recognition for Brando. *The New York Times'* Bosley Crowther said, "Director Elia Kazan and a simply superlative cast have fashioned a motion picture that throbs with passion and poignancy. Indeed, through the haunting performance England's great Vivien Leigh gives in the heart-breaking role of Mr. Williams deteriorating Southern belle and through the mesmerizing mood Mr. Kazan has wreathed with the techniques of the screen, this picture...now becomes as fine, if not finer, than the play. Inner torments are seldom projected with such sensitivity and clarity on the screen.

The *Times* critic added, "Of course, the first factor in this triumph is Mr. Williams' play, which embraces, among its many virtues, an essential human condition in visual terms. The last brave, defiant, hopeless struggle of the lonely and decaying Blanche Du Bois to hold on to her faded gentility against the heartless badgering of her roughneck brother-in-law is a tangible cat-and-dog set-to, marked with manifold physical episodes as well as a wealth of fluctuations of verbally fashioned images and moods."

Crowther considered Miss Leigh's performance brilliant and commented upon the great vitality and flexibility necessary for her role. But he continued, "No less brilliant, however, within his area is Marlon Brando in the role of the loud, lusty, brawling, brutal, amoral Polish brother-in-law. Mr. Brando created the role in the stage play and he carries over all the energy and the steel-spring characteristics that made him vivid on the stage. But here, where we're so much closer to him, he seems that much more highly charged, his despairs seem that much more pathetic and his comic moments that much more slyly enjoyed."

Kim Hunter, Brando.

Brando, Vivien Leigh.

Kim Hunter, Brando.

use the word, both had plot elements concerning abortion. *People Will Talk* had Cary Grant portraying a broadminded hero willing to marry a girl who is pregnant out of wedlock with another man's child.

Though the rape scene in *Streetcar* was toned down, it was still effective. Critics of the day also commented that the underlying sexual byplay combined with the hostility between Blanche and Kowalski was lost in the film version, since Blanche was made a more sympathetic character. When the character of Blanche is recalled, one remembers her classic line: "Whoever you are, I have always depended on the kindness of strangers."

Otis Guernsey, Jr., in the *New York Herald Tribune*, best summarized why Kowalski, and Brando's brilliant portrayal of him, dominated the film: "Being a part of this world, the brother-in-law played by Brando can be brought as close to reality as possible. Brando gives a

The underlying sexual attraction between Blanche and Kowalski was not as evident in the film as in the play.

Newsweek commented that Brando's "succinct inventory of Blanche's poor trunkful of finery is a masterpiece on Brando's part." They noted that he had the rare ability to be great among an excellent group of players. *Newsweek* also noted that the rape scene, explicit in the stage play, was somewhat less so in the film version.

Time said, "Within the limits of Hollywood's self-censoring production code, the movie followed the play's story faithfully." In Williams' play, there is no retribution for Kowalski's rape of Blanche. For the film version, Kazan had to agree to change the ending in order to get the rape scene by the censors. Kowalski's "punishment" was his wife's leaving him. However, as *Time* said, "this seems not only mild but temporary."

Other films that year also suggested a loosening of the self-censoring Hollywood production code. *Detective Story* and *A Place in the Sun*, although they did not remarkably truthful performance of a heavy-muscled, practical animal, secure in the normalcy of marriage and friendship, proud but indelicate, cunning but insensitive, aware of Blanche's deceits but not of her suffering. This performance is as close to perfect as one could wish, in every mannerism and inflection of voice Brando gives a brilliantly detailed impression of a rough-edged fellow reacting in what is accepted as the normal way and not to be blamed personally for not sympathizing with another person's obscure agonies."

Although the character of Stanley Kowalski was not a rebel, in *Streetcar* Brando firmly established the style and characteristics the rebel of the 1950s would follow—the mumbling, incoherent speech, the sensual scratching, the long pauses and intense stares. This was a direct change from the verbal Lower East Side John Garfield rebel and Clift's aloof, patrician rebel.

A Place in the Sun, Montgomery Clift's fifth movie, was released shortly after *Streetcar*. The two films, both now considered classics, vied for 1951's top Oscars. However, *An American in Paris* won as Best Picture, although George Stevens won as Best Director for *A Place in the Sun*.

A Place in the Sun was the second screen version (the first was made in 1931) of Theodore Dreiser's 1925 novel, *An American Tragedy*. Both versions were produced by Paramount. In the 1951 film, based on Patrick Kearney's play adapted from the novel, the time and setting was switched to the present. Instead of concentrating on the social aspects of the Dreiser novel, screenwriters Michael Wilson and Harry Brown (who won 1951 Academy Awards for Best Screenplay) focused on the story of the leading character, whose name they changed from Clyde Griffiths to George Eastman. Clift's introverted acting style, characterized by blank stares and perplexed expressions, was used to perfection by George Stevens to convey the character's inner conflict which resulted in his downfall.

It might be argued that Stevens gave only surface treatment to the society which propelled Eastman to his tragic end and emphasized his love affairs and groping for a higher rung on the social ladder. The Eastman character was portrayed as an intelligent youth whose background did not equip him for anything better than menial labor. So it wasn't surprising that he grasped at the chance to work in his rich uncle's factory. Ignored by his rich relatives, the lonely, brooding young man found companionship with a drab and equally lonely co-worker, Alice Tripp. Then the youth is suddenly exposed to the overwhelming affluence of his family and meets and falls in love with Angela Vickers. Because of

his basic upbringing—a combination of fanatic evangelism and the slum environment he longed to escape—he cannot callously desert Alice when she becomes pregnant. So he plots to remedy his situation by murdering her. This part of their ordeal is tastefully and compellingly handled. His intrinsic cowardice is sharply revealed when he cannot go through with the planned murder. Alice's accidental drowning and the subsequent mounting terror and confusion on the part of Eastman, who harbors the insidious thought that while he did not commit murder he must have willed it, was stunningly presented. Eastman, grappling with a sin he cannot fully comprehend, is pitiful yet strangely courageous explaining his act and his beliefs in the courtroom scenes.

Once again, Clift was presented with the role of a character filled with inner conflict. *The New York Times* noted, "There may be some belief that Montgomery Clift, as the tortured George Eastman, is not nearly the designing and grasping youth conceived by Dreiser. But his portrayal, often terse and hesitating, is full, rich, restrained, and, above all, generally credible and poignant. He is, in effect, a believable mama's boy gone wrong."

Critics also had great praise for Shelley Winters as the drab, tragic girl, and for Elizabeth Taylor as the socialite ingenue. Stevens' directorial touches were cited—for example, the way he subtly indicated that Clift and Winters had spent the night together.

Clift received his second Academy Award nomination for *A Place in the Sun*. Both he and Brando lost that year to Humphrey Bogart, who won for *The African Queen*.

Fan magazines exploited the friendship between Elizabeth Taylor and Clift and promoted them as America's sweethearts. Long after the magazine hoopla died away, their friendship remained steady.

A Place in the Sun was tremendously relevant to the youth of the early fifties. A new generation of soul-searchers reacted to the tormented hero portrayed by Clift. The liberated youth of the sixties and seventies would probably not be able to identify readily with George Eastman, a character caught up and eventually devoured by middle-class values. But youth of the fifties was turned on to his dilemma. He was a man rebelling against his fate without knowing how and questioning why. He was the rebel hero of the day.

Although this was Clift's fifth film and second Academy Award nomination, *A Place in the Sun* is the film which exemplifies his contribution to the rebel hero image. In 1958, seven years after the film was released, Dennis Hopper, who would become one of the leading rebels of the seventies, met Montgomery Clift for the first time. As if the picture had just been released,

Philip Holmes in the 1931 film of *An American Tragedy*,
re-made in 1951 as *A Place in the Sun*.

Elizabeth Taylor, Shepperd Strudwick as her father,
Montgomery Clift in *A Place in the Sun*.

Hopper told Clift how much he had been moved by his portrayal of George Eastman. Clift was shocked and hurt, since he had made half a dozen films since.

There was—and still is—a great controversy about who copied whom in the Clift-Brando style of acting. True, Clift was playing leading roles on Broadway long before Brando, but it is Brando who is known as the leading proponent of the Actors Studio method. Brando is credited with originating the "mumble-scratch" school of acting. But Clift did indeed originate the "blank stare-perplexed look" school. The question is moot, since Clift fans will argue that he was the forerunner, and Brando's fans, a larger and still vocal group, argue that every post-1950 screen rebel exists in Brando's shadow.

Though Clift was off-screen for a year, Brando had one film released in 1952, *Viva Zapata*. As he had researched his role for *The Men,* Brando now spent months studying Mexican history, researching the character of Emiliano Zapata. Once again, Elia Kazan was director. John Steinbeck wrote the screenplay, based on the novel *Viva Zapata* by Edgcumn Pinchon. Darryl F. Zanuck produced the film, the story of the agrarian rebel who was Pancho Villa's principal revolutionary confederate. It was another triumph for Zanuck and his studio, 20th Century-Fox, which was at the height of its postwar "message picture" boom.

The character Zapata was a revolutionary as well as being a rebel. Brando played the part with fervor, even transforming his features with special makeup and fake moustache to look amazingly like the guerilla leader. Anthony Quinn, as Zapata's boisterous warrior brother, Eufemio, gave an outstanding performance and won his first Oscar as Best Supporting Actor. Jean Peters portrayed the proper young lady of the village who falls in love with the wild man of the hills and marries him. She was the typical good girl foil for the rebel character.

Otis Guernsey in the *New York Herald Tribune* said: "Directed by Elia Kazan in strong moods of blood and fire, and acted by Marlon Brando in a smoldering saturnine portrayal of a man of violence, *Viva Zapata* studies the tricky relationship between the 'man on the horse' and the people who provide him with inspiration and enfranchise his acts."

Clift on witness stand.

Guernsey continued, "Zapata is presented as a hero in the sense that he possesses all the animal virtues and uses his strength only against injustice or treachery. But he is not polished out of all recognition as a human being; Brando gives his character all the rough edges and soiled spots of a half-civilized man whose spoken words are deceptively simple and whose demeanor is deceptively calm. In this, as well as in other respects, *Viva Zapata* binds good and bad together in a Chinese puzzle of harsh experience. It offers no easy moralities or solutions—its people are actually in worse state after Zapata's struggles, having been disillusioned and betrayed by each apparent political champion. But it suggested in Steinbeck's script that they are at last ready to shoulder their own individual responsibilities and need no longer depend on leaders."

The New York Times critic Crowther said, "His acting of a baffled, tongue-tied Indian does not carry too much force."

"But when this dynamic young performer is speaking his anger or his love for a fellow revolutionary, or when he is charging through the land at the head of his rebel-soldiers or walking bravely into the trap of his doom, there is power enough in his portrayal to cause the screen to throb. And throb it does, in particular, in the last tragic, heartbreaking scene, when the rebel leader is shot down, the victim of his own unfailing trust."

Time was the only major publication of the day to be more concerned with the historical inaccuracy of Steinbeck's script than with the impact of the movie, which they described as "a good, muscular horse opera."

Many critics could not help but compare Brando's performance in *Zapata* to his two previous screen roles. "In Marlon Brando's brooding Zapata—mandarin moustache and all—," said *Newsweek*, "there is a hint of Kowalski in 'Streetcar' and the sullen Wilozek of 'The Men.' But beyond that there is a careful and intelligent characterization of the humanitarian who was wise

JOHN STEINBECK'S
VIVA ZAPATA!

STARRING
MARLON BRANDO · JEAN PETERS

20th CENTURY-FOX

PRODUCED BY
DARRYL F. ZANUCK

DIRECTED BY
ELIA KAZAN

WRITTEN BY
JOHN STEINBECK

with ANTHONY QUINN · JOSEPH WISEMAN · ARNOLD MOSS · ALAN REED · MARGO · HAROLD GORDON · LOU GILBERT · MILDRED DUNNOCK

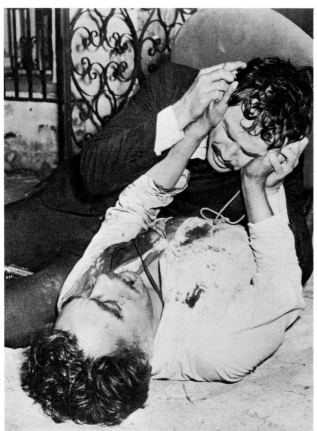

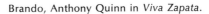
Brando, Anthony Quinn in *Viva Zapata.*

Brando in *Viva Zapata.*

enough to know that no nation could survive in the shadow of a single leader."

Viva Zapata was shot on location in Texas, near the Rio Grande. Many Mexican actors were used as extras, including a still beautiful woman, Maria Casteneda, who had achieved brief celebrity seventeen years earlier when, known as Movita, she played the native girl in MGM's 1935 production, *Mutiny on the Bounty.*

Brando and Movita established a relationship which would be sporadic over the next ten years but would eventually culminate in marriage.

For *Zapata,* Brando was nominated for his third consecutive Oscar, but Gary Cooper won for *High Noon.*

In May 1952, John Garfield died in New York. He was thirty-nine. During the last months of his life, he had been waging an unsuccessful battle to redeem himself in the eyes of the film industry, the press, and the public. For eighteen months, he had been unable to get a role in Hollywood or on Broadway, until he did a nine-week revival of *Golden Boy* in the spring of 1952. That year both Elia Kazan and Clifford Odets, whom many thought Garfield was protecting in some of his evasive testimony, went before the House Un-American Activities Com-

Brando as Emiliano Zapata.

mittee and confessed their past Communist associations. Under FBI investigation, Garfield, just prior to his death, was working on a statement, with the help of Arnold Foster of the Anti-Defamation League, going over his alleged discrepancies in his testimony and admitting that he lied to the Committee about his former affiliations. He never held a party card, he said, but described how "an emotional and sentimental" Hollywood actor could be drawn unwittingly into the Communist web. He admitted that they had gotten him into thirty-two red front organizations, and persuaded him to sign forty-two petitions. But Garfield never finished the statement.

He had also composed a letter to Spyros Skouras, then President of 20th Century-Fox, attempting to get the lead role in a film called *Taxi*, a role which eventually went to Dan Dailey. The part would have been perfect for Garfield—the character was a tough misogynist, an enterprising hackie waging a singlehanded battle against the world who becomes involved in a sentimental story of a young mother in search of her husband.

Also, Garfield had been working on a magazine article

Dan Dailey got the role in *Taxi* that Garfield desperately wanted.

abjuring Communism. Supposedly, sixteen pages of this manuscript still exist.

During this period, Garfield quarreled with his wife. Theirs had been a stormy relationship, and many said that she was opposed to his abjuring Communism. On May 10, Garfield left Roberta and took up residence in a Manhattan hotel. Ten days later, after dining with actress Iris Whitney, he returned with her to her apartment at 3 Gramercy Park. Miss Whitney's version of ensuing events: he complained of feeling ill, but refused an offer to call a doctor; he went to sleep in her bedroom; she, not wishing to disturb him, slept on the couch in her living room; in the morning she found him dead. The staid *New York Times* ran a headline: "Garfield Found Dead in the Home of a Friend." But New York tabloids ran more colorful headlines, and readers' imaginations were encouraged.

Time reported, "One day last week three cops, summoned by a doctor who had already made his report, forced open the door of a Gramercy Park apartment. Inside stood a blonde ex-actress who sobbed that her dinner companion of the night before had complained of feeling "awful" and had come to her place to rest. Behind her in the bedroom lay the body of John Garfield. After thirty-nine years, the tough guy's heart had given up."

Garfield had had mild heart attacks in 1949 and 1951, and had been warned to take it easy. The Communist party and its followers immediately claimed that his third and fatal heart attack was the result of "persecution" by the House Committee on Un-American Activities.

Although depressed and out of work, the Dead End Kid from the Lower East Side who made it in the movies did not die penniless. Garfield left his wife and children a gross estate of nearly $250,000.

Garfield's sudden death was a shock to the public. An estimated 10,000 people, mostly women, attended his funeral. *Newsweek* said, "Not since the death of screen idol Rudolph Valentino has there been such a public display of grief over a film personality."

Garfield's legacy included the rebel hero character.

4

The Golden Years of the Rebel Hero

"If a man don't go his own way, he's nothin'," said Montgomery Clift as Private Robert E. Lee Prewitt in *From Here to Eternity*. This philosophy, the character of Prewitt and Clift's portrayal captured the imagination of millions of moviegoers in Fred Zinnemann's 1953 film of James Jones' best-selling novel.

Throughout his life, Clift "went his own way" and made his own career decisions. After *A Place in the Sun* in 1951, the actor and Paramount mutually terminated their remaining one-picture commitment. The reason given was "lack of a suitable role." However, Paramount and director George Stevens, who had used Clift so bril-

liantly in *A Place in the Sun*, then produced *Shane*, one of the screen's classic Westerns, with a title role perfectly suited to Clift's talents. Alan Ladd was acceptable as the anti-hero gunfighter Shane, who aids homesteaders Van Heflin and Jean Arthur. But one cannot help contemplate how much more effective the interplay might have been between Shane and the homesteader's child (Brandon de Wilde) if Clift had played the role. And Clift's sensitivity (vs. Ladd's cold handsomeness) would have aided in the suggestions of sexual attraction between Shane and Jean Arthur.

Clift had returned to the screen early in 1953 for

Alfred Hitchcock in *I Confess*. That film had an intriguing premise but Hitchcock was forced by the production code to compromise in its execution. Clift portrayed a Canadian priest accused of murder. The priest couldn't reveal the identity of the real killer because the murderer had confessed his crime to him, and the sanctity of the confessional is absolute.

Clift's friends often compared him to a priest or a monk because the actor took ascetic measures during a film's production. When Clift accepted the role in *I Confess*, the script called for the priest to be hanged in the end, and then proven innocent. But the Hollywood censors insisted that this would offend Catholics, so the ending was changed and the real murderer was revealed in the nick of time. For a love interest, the story included a flashback love affair with Anne Baxter prior to Clift's entering the priesthood.

I Confess was both a critical and box-office disappointment. But some reviewers noted that Clift's "underplaying" was perfect for his role as a man forced to keep his own counsel lest he betray his highest ideals.

In July 1953, what most people consider Clift's best film, *From Here to Eternity*, was released. Once again Zinnemann, who had directed Clift in *The Search*, used the actor to achieve precisely the right combination of intensity and casualness.

From Here to Eternity, with an all-star cast headed by Clift, Burt Lancaster, Deborah Kerr, Donna Reed, Frank Sinatra and Ernest Borgnine, was filmed at Columbia's Hollywood studios and on location in Hawaii. It was brought in for $2 million, and grossed over $12 million in the United States alone.

The sprawling plot concerned pre-World War II professional Army life in Hawaii. The character of Prewitt represented the stubborn individualist caught up in the politics of army life. Clift, basically a passive actor, was ideally cast as a man who was a shock absorber for society's insensitivity. In this film, Clift was the ultimate rebel hero of the screen up to this time—possessing individualism and pride, refusing to bend to the will of society, but not attempting to change it. He fought forces from both within and without. He was a loner with a streak of nobility, combining sensitivity, virility and innate intelligence. The audience immediately sympathized and identified.

Time said Prewitt was the "man who cannot play it smart because he is cursed with a piece of ultimate wisdom," referring to his line, "If a man don't go his own way, he's nothin'."

The reviewers all commented on Zinnemann's and screenwriter Daniel Taradash's ability to transpose the multi-themed novel to the screen. *Newsweek* said, "A number of people have taken a bawdy behemoth of a book that affronted good taste, morals, and the United States Army, and have nursed it intelligently between the Scylla and Charybdis of the Johnston office and the Pentagon.

"Produced at a time when Hollywood is preoccupied with escapism, and even busier escaping from itself with 3-D gadgetry, *From Here to Eternity* is a grown-up movie . . . a castful of players act with the realization that they are working in a film that demands intelligence and a complete understanding of the complex characters involved.

Newsweek added, "In cutting Jones' novel from 861 pages to a shooting script of 164, Taradash has also eliminated the clinical sex stuff that Jones found an important part of his Army life. The scenes of brutality in a Hawaiian stockade are suggested rather than bludgeoned on the line, and if the life of the professional, thirty-year soldier is a rugged one, it is hereby the fault of the neurotic individual rather than an indictment of the

Alan Ladd, Brandon de Wilde in *Shane*.
The boy is awed by Shane's expertise and anti-hero attitudes. Shane was a role suited to Clift's talents.

Army system. There are other script concessions for propriety's sake: The New Congress Club, in Honolulu, has become 'a sort of primitive USO, a place of well-worn merriment. It is not a house of prostitution'..."

The scenes at the New Congress Club and Donna Reed's performance were, however, so effective, that there was never any doubt why the soldiers frequented the establishment. Miss Reed justifiably won the Oscar for Best Supporting Actress.

The film concentrated more on Prewitt than the book had. And, as *Newsweek* noted, the emphasis changed from the system's corrosive effect on individuals to an individual's ability to cope with the system.

Otis Guernsey in the *New York Herald Tribune* said that "the adaptation and concise direction built up a thunderhead of fatality over Prewitt's story. Visible in brute faces and brusque army routine, and symbolized musically in the pulsating sadness of a bugle blowing 'Taps,' this fatality carries the film over its weak spots in a compelling paradox of personal disaster.

"Those who have read the book will remember that Prewitt was what the movie euphemistically calls a 'hard-head.' Played by Montgomery Clift with slim, muscular efficiency and deep-set, brooding eyes, Prewitt commits himself to perfection—that is his tragedy. Loving the Army and excellent at his job whether it be bulging or soldiering, he is nevertheless committed to the kind of rugged individualism which has no resilience

Clift in the confessional as the priest in Hitchcock's *I Confess*.

Montgomery Clift, Burt Lancaster, Frank Sinatra in *From Here to Eternity*. Sinatra and Clift became off-screen buddies.

Frank Sinatra, Clift in *From Here to Eternity*. Sinatra's role almost went to Eli Wallach.

for injustice, humiliation or any but the physical strains of Army life.

"Thus," concluded Guernsey, "he sows the seeds of his own demise, because the Army is not perfect; it has officers like Philip Ober as the company commander who values athletic trophies above his soldiers' rights. It has non-coms who give Prewitt 'the treatment' in field maneuvers when he refuses to join the boxing team. The fact that these unjust persons eventually get their come-uppance from headquarters does not muffle novelist Jones's cry of indignation that the Army can be a tough, unsympathetic and cruel place even in peace time. Zinnemann stages this indignation in short, vicious jabs of action and talk in the barracks, in training and even in the bedroom. Here regimentation is derailed and out of control, a scary monster in everything from silent suffering to a bloody fist fight."

Everyone concerned with *From Here to Eternity* received superlative reviews. *The New York Times* said, "Montgomery Clift adds another sensitive portrait to his already imposing gallery." The *New York Herald Tribune* said, "Clift's version of Prewitt is both taut and sensitive, as he takes what is dished out to him, suppresses his love for the bugle except for one ringing 'Taps' and

Montgomery Clift, Donna Reed. Usually a "good girl," she won an Oscar for her change-of-pace performance as a prostitute in *From Here to Eternity*.

Sinatra fights Ernest Borgnine in *From Here to Eternity*.

transfers his emotions to a pretty prostitute. He makes himself indigestible to the Army, almost willfully, but he always has sympathy on his side even in an occasion of murder."

Time said, referring to Clift, Lancaster and Sinatra, "The three male leads in the film turn in the finest performances of their careers. Montgomery Clift displays a marvelous snail-like capacity to contract his feeling and intelligence into the close little shell of Prew's personality, and yet he also manages to convey that within this very limited man blazes a large spirit."

"This is what Hollywood calls 'a big picture,' " continued *Time*, "loaded with 'production values.' And yet, *From Here to Eternity* also tries to be something more. It tries to tell a truth about life, about the inviolability of the human spirit, and in some measure it fails. Yet the picture does succeed, perhaps without quite intending to, in saying something important about America. It says that many Americans, in a way that is often confused and sometimes forgotten, care to the quick about a man's right to 'go his own way,' though all the world and the times be contrary."

A man who had gone his own way in the late forties and early fifties was Frank Sinatra, not yet a screen rebel but certainly one of the leading off-screen rebels in the entire history of show business.

After a meteoric career as band singer, bobby-sox idol, and movie star in musicals, by 1952 Frank Sinatra couldn't get a job in Hollywood. His record sales had slumped, he temporarily lost his voice, his boy-next-door public image was shattered when he left his wife and children for a tempestuous affair and marriage to love goddess Ava Gardner, and MGM had dropped him from their roster.

When Sinatra sought the role of Angelo Maggio in *From Here to Eternity*, Miss Gardner had to buy his plane ticket to Hollywood (he had accompanied her to Africa where she was filming *Mogambo*). Back in Hollywood he had to undergo the humiliation of a screen test for the part. Eli Wallach was the favorite, and Columbia studio boss Harry Cohn was initially opposed to Sinatra. Sinatra got the role, but his salary was only $8000, a staggering drop from his usual $150,000 per picture.

Maggio, a temperamental, lust-for-life Italian-American GI, undergoes the injustices of the Army, unbending, and is eventually killed by the sadistic sergeant (played by Ernest Borgnine) who runs the Army stockade.

For his remarkably sensitive performance, especially his death scene in Clift's arms, Sinatra won unanimous critical raves. "Frank Sinatra does Private Maggio like nothing he has ever done before," wrote *Time*. "His face wears the calm of a man who is completely sure of what he is doing as he plays it straight from Little Italy.

And Ernest Borgnine is a Fatso hard to forget. He can smile and smile and he is a villain, in a way to make the audience realize that it is in the presence of that perhaps not rarest of humankind, the perfectly normal monster."

Sinatra won back the respect of the industry and the public, who could now consider him a serious actor as well as a song-and-dance man. And he won the Academy Award for Best Supporting Actor.

Sinatra as Maggio, and in a few subsequent roles, represented a certain realistic rebel of the screen which many could identify with. He was a throwback to the Garfield rebel of the Depression—verbal, wisecracking, on occasion physically violent. *From Here to Eternity* reestablished Sinatra as a major star, and it drew millions into theatres at a time when America wasn't going to the movies. It won seven Academy Awards, including Best Picture, Best Director and Best Screenplay.

Interestingly enough, the Navy banned the film from its ships and bases, although the Army and Air Force did not.

Eternity was Clift's seventh film. Although he would make ten more films in the next thirteen years, he would never again reach the heights of *From Here to Eternity*. He received his third—and last—Academy Award nomination as Best Actor.

Clift was momentarily the screen's leading rebel. In 1953, *Julius Caesar*, starring Brando as Mark Antony, was released and Clift and Brando again vied for the Oscar. However, William Holden won for *Stalag 17*.

Julius Caesar was directed by Joseph Mankiewicz. It had an MGM all-star cast including James Mason, Deborah Kerr, Greer Garson, Louis Calhern, Edmond O'Brien, and John Gielgud. It was Brando's fourth film, and netted him his fourth consecutive Oscar nomination.

When signed for the role of Mark Antony, there was much speculation as to whether Brando would play the role as an offshoot of Messrs. Wilozek-Kowalski. Jokes circulated on the supposed delivery of the "Friends, Romans, Countrymen" speech. Brando, however, surprised everyone. His interpretation of Antony was articulate, restrained but intense. It proved what a really fine actor he was, and that he could perform Shakespeare with consummate technique.

Bosley Crowther said, "The delight and surprise of the film is Mr. Brando's 'Mark Antony' . . . happily, Mr. Brando's diction, which had been guttural and slurred in previous films, is clear and precise in this instance. In him, a major talent has emerged."

Although performing Shakespeare, Brando's innate sensuality came through. As Otis Guernsey in the *New York Herald Tribune* noted, "Marlon Brando's Antony is constrained and studied in its details, but it has an animal vigor that bursts forth when needed."

Marlon Brando was not to be denied his place as the leading screen rebel of the 1950's. Following *Julius Caesar*, his next two films—*The Wild One*, released in December, 1953, and *On the Waterfront*, released in 1954—cemented his position as super-star and rebel.

When a character in *The Wild One* asks Brando what he's rebelling against, he asks back, "What have you got?" Brando created an unforgettable portrait as the tough black leather-jacketed leader of a motorcycle gang in this, one of the most controversial films ever made. The gang appropriately calls itself the Black Rebels. After being ordered out of a nearby motorcycle meet, the Black Rebel motorcycle "club" wheels into the symbolic little American town of Wrightsville. The "club" is virtually an outlaw gang, and from the beginning they look for trouble. In the inadequately policed little town, it isn't long before a good deal of hell is being raised. When the town's citizens form a vigilante committee to retaliate, things become more volatile.

Brando becomes involved with the 1953 version of Priscilla Lane. This time portrayed by Mary Murphy, the good, clean, upright small-town girl is the local waitress and daughter of the local, cowardly cop. Brando falls in love with her. Despite herself, she responds to his animal sex appeal and senses in him a gentleness and sensitivity which he himself is loathe to reveal.

Note the similarity between this relationship and those of the early Garfield-Priscilla Lane films. The difference, and this is what made the film and Brando controversial, is that by this time movies were beginning to show—and not just imply—the violence and sexuality these rebel characters possessed.

There is a drag race, an overturned car, a brawling fight between Brando and Lee Marvin, the leader of a rival gang, and finally an accidental killing. Brando is accused, but cleared through the help of the girl and her father.

The script was based on a short story "The Cyclist's Raid" by Frank Rooney, in turn based on an actual event in the late 1940s, when thousands of members of a motorcycle club held a riotous convention in a small California town. The film was produced by Stanley Kramer, directed by Laslo Benedek, with a screenplay by John Paxton. The plot of the film is not what is important—it is the theme and mood of the picture which made it one of the most talked-about films of the early fifties. *The Wild One* set the tone for the next twenty years of films about youth gangs and motorcyclists.

Unlike the short story, which made no attempt to analyze why the young men acted the way they did but merely drew a parallel between their destructiveness and the destructiveness of Hitler Youth and other such

Brando as Marc Antony, with Louis Calhern as Caesar and Greer Garson as Calpurnia in MGM's *Julius Caesar*.

Brando delivers the famous "Friends, Romans, Countrymen" speech.

Brando and gang in *The Wild One*.

groups, the film honestly tried to explore the underlying problems that produced these social misfits.

However, the film never states what the sources are, and it may have failed in its attempt as a social drama with significance, since most people remember it as a movie about violence. Even Brando has been quoted as expressing his unhappiness with the final picture: "We started out to explain the hipster psychology, but somewhere along the way we went off the track. The result was that instead of finding out why young people tend to bunch into groups that seek expression in violence, all we did was show the violence."

The Wild One received mixed reviews. The national magazines, including *Time* and *Newsweek*, seemed to hit at the film for being "violent for violence's sake." But Bosley Crowther said, "So long as the makers of this picture permit it to stay in the realm of graphic examination of the behavior and depredations of this mob, it is a powerful and terrifying survey. And when they wryly rush up the weak reserves of a normal and baffled community in the form of one cowardly cop and a snarling handful of vigilantes, they briefly project their film onto the elevated level of social drama with significance and scope. . . . Withal, *The Wild One* is a picture of extra-

ordinary candor and courage—a picture that tries to grasp an idea, even though its reach falls short."

Other critics noted that it was a study of what a group of uncontrolled hoodlums could do to a small town; what the townspeople, when roused to counteraction, could do to propel the situation to an inevitable tragedy, and vividly portrayed both the early ineffectualness and the ultimate healing power of reasonableness when confronted with force.

Brando's performance was one of intensity and brooding and received generally good reviews. This was the first film in which Brando portrayed the rebel with outward bravado but inner hurt. You could see that underneath his swaggering pose he was just a crazy, mixed-up boy searching for something to rebel against. One glowing insight into the character of Johnny was provided when, while being beaten up by the town's citizens, he manages to snarl, "My old man hit harder than that."

As the protagonist in *The Wild One*, Brando has no code, only instincts. Johnny and the motorcycle gang appealed to the youth of the fifties because they vocally and physically opposed authority. They were saying and doing the things that all the youngsters who saw the film had thought of saying and doing.

Brando tangles with rival gang leader Lee Marvin.

In the fifties (as today) in Europe, filmmakers and audiences were more concerned with censoring violence than sex. In England, *The Wild One* was considered a dangerous film that could possibly incite youth to riot. Even in America, where censors have always been primarily concerned with censoring sex, and violence on screen has been treated leniently, *The Wild One* was considered a particularly violent film. The critics were divided. Many thought that Hollywood had done a service in making a film about the grotesque events in the news and trying to shock the public into an awareness of the youth unrest to come.

The sexuality possessed by the rebel, only hinted at in the Garfield-Priscilla Lane relationships, was now becoming overt. It was quite obvious, even to the most naive moviegoer, what Brando had in mind as he roughly tugged Mary Murphy's chin. Sexuality was emerging. Even the violence in the film was a form of sexuality, and the cyclists gunning their motors and riding in ritualistic group patterns make it clear, along with their dialogue, that they live for sensations.

However, it was only 1953 and so our hero, having been helped by the good girl who succeeded in unearthing some feelings of sensitivity, rides off into the sunrise alone. Brando had made the torn T-shirt a sex symbol in 1951. Now, in 1954, the black leather jacket and motorcycles became symbols of virility. (Although he did become a cycle enthusiast off-screen, Brando did not do his own riding in the picture.)

Both at the height of their rebel images, Clift and Brando appealed to different types. Brando's characters had no code. *The Wild One* begins with an empty road behind the titles and a bit of narrative read by Brando: "Once the trouble was on the way, I just went along with it." And the Brando character was not intellectual. He could not rationalize, accept things, live with them,

as could Clift in *From Here to Eternity*. In *The Wild One* Brando could only feel, act and be the rebel. Each actor found his audience. There were the tough, delinquent rebels who followed Brando, and the strong personal code rebels who empathized with Clift. Both actors were vulnerable, both had "little boy" qualities, both needed protection and both, like Garfield before them, were eternal outsiders.

Brando's sixth film, *On the Waterfront*, was released during the summer of 1954. The idea for a film about union corruption among New York dock workers supposedly dates back to the late forties, when Elia Kazan and Arthur Miller talked about collaboration on a story. After Kazan had testified before the House Un-American Activities Committee, his friendship with Miller cooled, and the idea was abandoned, but not forgotten.

Townspeople attack motorcycle club leader Brando in *The Wild One*.

Brando arrested in accidental slaying in *The Wild One*. Note his unwillingness to attempt communicating with the establishment. Also note the good girl's longing to aid him.

Brando, Mary McCarthy in *The Wild One*. Sexuality was emerging.

Reporter Malcolm Johnson won a Pulitzer Prize for a series of articles for the now defunct *New York Sun* about murder and racketeering in the New York waterfront union, and in 1950 screenwriter Budd Schulberg began writing a screenplay based on the articles. Three years later, Schulberg and Kazan began collaborating on the project, and approached Sam Spiegel to produce the film.

From the onset, Kazan wanted Brando for the lead. But Brando was unavailable due to other commitments, so Spiegel supposedly promised the role to Frank Sinatra. Sinatra, hot on the comeback trail with *From Here to Eternity,* seemed right for the role of the aging, punch-drunk ex-fighter.

After *Viva Zapata* at Fox, Brando contracted to star for the studio in *The Egyptian.* After reading the script, he conveniently disappeared. Newspaper columnists reported "Brando Lost" and headlines screamed, "Studio Suing Rebel Brando." Fox, in fact, sued Brando for two million dollars. (Eventually the case was settled out of court. Edmond Purdom got the role. The film was a financial disappointment.) Brando became available for Kazan and *On the Waterfront.* Reportedly, Sinatra was furious with Spiegel, and did not speak with him for years.

Brando, as he had with the role of Stanley Kowalski, made the role of Terry Malloy so much his own that it is now inconceivable that anyone else could possibly have played the part.

He received his fifth consecutive Academy Award

In the early fifties Brando was the violent, tough rebel —   Clift, the aloof, personal code rebel.

nomination for his performance as the tough but gentle knockabout who must fight the syndicate, in which his brother is a key figure, to maintain his dignity and integrity. Once again, it is the love of a sweet, innocent girl which provides the rebel character with the fortitude necessary to overcome the forces oppressing him.

In addition to Kazan, Schulberg, Spiegel, Leonard Bernstein making his debut as a movie composer, and Boris Kaufman as cinematographer, the film had a top-notch cast. Besides Brando there were Karl Malden, Lee J. Cobb, Rod Steiger, Leif Erickson, and a charming newcomer, New York actress Eva Marie Saint, in the role of the heroic heroine.

The story of *On the Waterfront* concerns an ex-prize-fighter, Terry Malloy (Brando), an errand boy for a crooked labor leader (Cobb). Malloy is tolerated because his brother (Steiger) is Cobb's lawyer. When one of his errands is used as bait to kill a fellow pigeon fancier who is about to testify before the crime commission, Terry becomes involved with the corruption that surrounds him. He meets and falls in love with the dead man's sister (Eva Marie Saint). Because of his streak of independence and nobility, his love for her, and the urgings of a crusading priest (Malden), Terry joins their cause.

After he is subpoenaed to testify before the crime commission, he is slated for death. In an unforgettable scene, while his brother is taking him by taxi to his execution, Brando delivers his now classic lines: "Oh Charlie, oh Charlie . . . you didn't understand. I coulda had class. I coulda been a contender. I coulda been somebody instead of a bum—which is what I am."

Steiger lets him escape and in turn he himself is murdered by the mob. Terry finds his brother's body hanging on a stevedore's hook. He then testifies before the crime commission and returns to the docks, where he beats up the labor boss. Although he is severely beaten in the process, he wins, and leads his friends back to work. The union bosses' hold has been broken.

The film and Brando received unanimous critical raves. *Newsweek* said, "It is difficult to imagine a role—except possibly that of Kowalski in 'Streetcar'—that is better suited to his [Brando's] particular talents."

Saturday Review said, "Brando's performance in this role is a piece of genuine artistry. With half-sentences finished by body shrugs and fish gestures of the hands, with a drawn-brow grasping for words, with a street arab's laugh or quick insult, with an ex-athlete's bounce to his walk, Brando projects a wonderfully absorbing portrait of a semi-stupid, stubborn, inner-sweet young man."

Otis Guernsey said, "Brando is crude and defiant as a young ex-boxer, a pet of the racketeers, who is nevertheless troubled by something roughly resembling a conscience. He ranges across the docks, the alleys and the rooftops like a half-tamed brute, uneasy in the jungle but barred from civilization. He uses his voice like a fist and concentrates aggression into every movement.

"Even when he is stung by the logic of the priest or staggered by the pale, chaste charm of Eva Marie Saint as the girl next door, he makes surrender seem like an aggressive act. This role bursts out of Brando with instinctive energy and startling accuracy, in a performance which is a show in itself."

The New York Times said, "Marlon Brando's Terry Malloy is a shatteringly poignant portrait of an amoral, confused, illiterate citizen of the lower depths who is goaded into decency by love, hate and murder. His groping for words, use of the vernacular, care of his beloved pigeons, pugilist's walk and gestures and his discoveries of love and the immensity of the crimes surrounding him are highlights of a beautiful and moving portrayal."

Time, always reluctant to admit near-perfection, conceded: "Brando in this show is one glorious meathead. The gone look, the reet vocabulary and the sexual arrogance are still the Brando brand of behavior. But for once the mannerisms converge, like symptoms, to point out the nature of the man who has them. The audience may never forget that Brando is acting, but it will know that he is doing a powerful acting job.

"Beside this almost massive performance, the others, even though good, seem a little small. Rod Steiger, as the brother, is, to the life, the kind of Irish bright boy who can get a little too smart for himself. Eva Marie Saint is quite right, too, in her convent-kept freshness, as the kind of narrow little good girl the bad boys long to be redeemed by. Karl Malden is bulldoggish as the priest, but hardly conveys the earthy sagacity of the living models the part was drawn from.

"The excellent acting, however, is surpassed by Boris Kaufman's photography."

On the Waterfront was a gigantic commercial as well as critical hit. Brando finally won the Oscar as Best Actor. Eva Marie Saint won as Best Supporting Actress, Elia Kazan for Best Director, and the film won as Best Picture. In addition, Boris Kaufman won an Oscar for his cinematography, Budd Schulberg for story and screenplay.

There is a theory that *On the Waterfront* is Schulberg and Kazan's defense of their positions on informing. Each testified before the House Un-American Activities Committee. Arthur Miller's play and subsequent movie, *View From the Bridge* (1962), also has this underlying theme on informing. In *On the Waterfront* informing is good, in *View From the Bridge* it is bad. Miller had refused to testify before the Committee, and for some time was estranged from Kazan. However, in the sixties,

Brando insisted on authentic makeup for all his roles.

Brando, Eva Marie Saint in *On the Waterfront*. The ex-fighter buys the parochial school girl her first beer.

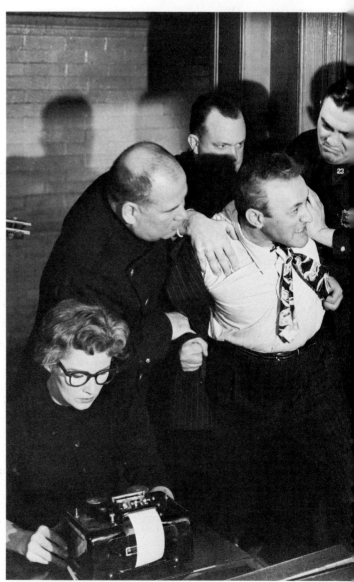

Rod Steiger, Brando in the famous
"Brother Charley" scene in *On the Waterfront*.

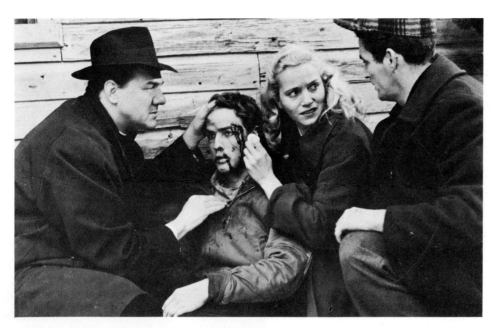

Karl Malden, Brando, Eva Marie Saint.

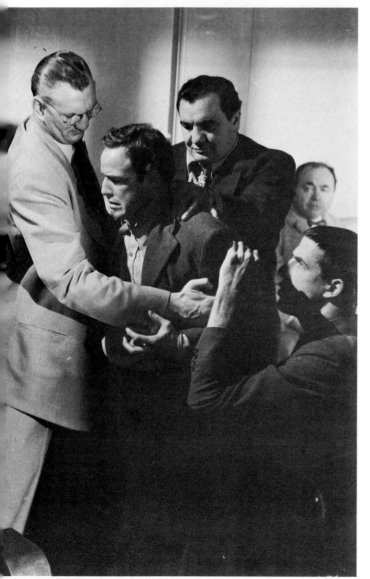

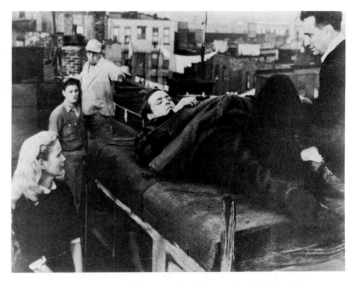

Kazan directing Brando, Eva Marie Saint.

Lee J. Cobb, Brando have a heated "discussion" in *On the Waterfront*.

Kazan directed Miller's play, *After the Fall*, which many people felt, and which Miller vehemently denies, was the story of his life with Marilyn Monroe.

In the days when Hollywood was promoting Cinema-Scope, Cinerama and 3-D, Kazan, Spiegel, Schulberg and Brando had collaborated to bring forth *On the Waterfront*, a black-and-white film that combined commercial success, social significance and artistic value.

Lee Rogow in *Saturday Review* said, "*On the Waterfront* will undoubtedly create a storm of excitement because of its use of the screen and because of Brando's vitalizing performance. I suspect that among the viewers there will be many who will find the ending somewhat pat and preachy and the plotting a bit slick. . . . But despite 'Waterfront's' shortcomings, there is no doubt that a landmark in American movie-making has been established by this documentary of the docks."

Much was written about the love scenes between Brando and Saint. They managed to create a totally genuine mood of deep sensitivity. Terry Malloy, like other Kazan heroes and most of the rebel heroes of the screen, lacked ambition, was set apart from his peers but had profound reserves of personal pride and integrity.

Although Brando would not undertake another rebel role for years, and indeed would try to change his screen image, *The Wild One* and *On the Waterfront* would keep him in the minds of moviegoers and critics as the unforgettable rebel.

Although he had missed the top rebel role of the decade, Sinatra did play a rebel that year. The role that had made John Garfield a star was rewritten in 1954 to suit Frank Sinatra's talents and capitalize on his new image, born in *From Here to Eternity*.

Titled *Young at Heart*, the musical re-make of *Four Daughters* co-starred Doris Day in the Priscilla Lane role and Gig Young in the Jeffrey Lynn part. Liam O'Brien adapted the original screenplay.

Sinatra had played his first—and only—villain that year, in the independent production *Suddenly*, a United Artists release. He portrayed a psychopathic would-be presidential assassin. *Young at Heart* returned Sinatra to a hero role, albeit a rebel hero with songs. The title of the film was borrowed from one of Sinatra's popular songs of the day and had no relation to the plot; he sang it over the opening and closing credits.

In general, *Young at Heart* received mixed reviews, but Sinatra and Day received strong personal notices. They worked well together, but the impact of the film was dulled by tacking on a happy ending (the 1938 ending had been realistic) whereby the Sinatra character does not succeed in committing suicide.

Bosley Crowther in *The New York Times* said, "Mr. Sinatra does put quills on the misfit before they blunt

Sinatra re-created the Garfield role of an itinerant piano player in *Young at Heart,* the musical re-make of *Four Daughters.*

Doris Day was top-billed over Sinatra in *Young at Heart.* Notice the same cookie-making scene as in the original Garfield film.

him to conformance in the end. Likewise Miss Day is attractive when she casually bounces around, before she becomes a soulsaver and one-girl society for the prevention of cruelty to strays."

While the *Times* was generally favorable toward the film, Bill Zinsser in the *New York Herald Tribune* said, "Even people who don't like Frank Sinatra will welcome his first entrance in *Young at Heart,* a movie so long as to be a double feature in itself—or so it seems. Sinatra first appears after about forty minutes, and then we are less than one-third through the syrupy musical.

"He walks into a home which is so relentlessly happy and American that it's almost a parody. It has a pipe-smoking Pop and a beloved old Aunt Jessie (Ethel Barrymore). It has three blond, blue-eyed daughters just full of cheer and locked-in goodness, and two of them have amiable oafs for boy friends. It has a dog and lace curtains, and the family conversation is the most adorable thing you've ever heard. My, every one of them is so nice!

"Then enter Sinatra. Good old Frankie. That morose face, that crooked smile, that sloppy posture, those hol-low eyes—all are a pleasure to behold. When he drags on a cigarette, you know he's enjoying it all for its rich, full, injurious flavor. And when he insists that life isn't always yummy and full of sunshine—why, land sakes, everybody thinks he's such a scamp.

"This family will make him happy even if it kills him, and it very nearly does. The next-to-last scene shows Frankie being wheeled into the operating room. And the last scene? Well, does this sound like a movie with a sad ending? That would be like putting bitters on jello."

The film played at the Paramount Theatre, and *The New York Times* said, "Sinatra croons some rueful ballads in that sultry voice that is still one of the best in the business. He is no longer the dreamy boy who packed this same Paramount Theatre with swooning bobby-soxers a decade ago, but he's a real actor now and he has outgrown musicals like *Young at Heart.* So have a good many moviegoers."

Rebel Sinatra's next film would star him with super-rebel Brando. Both had non-rebel roles in the dull film musical, *Guys and Dolls.*

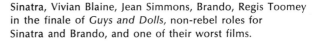

Sinatra as the Presidential assassin in *Suddenly.* It was one of his few villain roles.

Sinatra, Vivian Blaine, Jean Simmons, Brando, Regis Toomey in the finale of *Guys and Dolls,* non-rebel roles for Sinatra and Brando, and one of their worst films.

5
Dean—the Ultimate Rebel

1955 and 1956 were the golden years of the American screen rebel. The youth of the country had reacted strongly to the young, uncommunicative characters portrayed by screen newcomer James Dean.

Youth in every era is confronted with conflicting desires to conform to its peer group and yet be individual. Youth of the middle fifties had particular problems. Father figure Eisenhower was in the White House, the Senate Committee hearings on Communism had left the country with a vague feeling of uneasiness, and post-World War II affluence had further estranged parents and children. Depression children were now parents of teen-

agers of the 1950s. Parents who had experienced the deprivations of the Depression imbued their children with materialistic ideals. The youngsters, not oppressed with economic hardships or war, had time to be concerned with the lack of ethics and morals, the emptiness, indeed the hypocrisy, of their parents' lives.

The hero to youth was the teenager who appeared to conform yet successfully rebelled against conformity— and got away with it. James Dean not only did this, he also became so rich and successful that he could call the shots. He thereby combined the teenage dream— nonconformity—with the American dream—financial

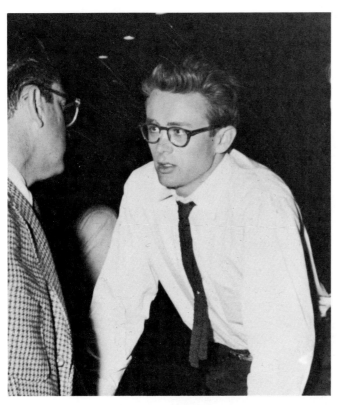

James Dean was seldom photographed wearing his glasses.

Tab Hunter, James Dean on the set of *Rebel Without a Cause*.

success—and was the envy and idol of the youth of his generation. They identified with him. After his death, they worshipped him.

When one realizes that the Dean legend has lived for more than fifteen years, it is amazing to think that James Dean spent less than two years as a star in Hollywood and made only three starring vehicles: *East of Eden*, *Rebel Without a Cause*, and *Giant*.

For the youth of the middle fifties, Dean was a symbol of loneliness, anger, and frustration. His screen image was a strong reflection of his personal life.

Dean was born of middle-class parents in Fairmont, Indiana, on February 8, 1931. Like Brando, he seemingly led a conventional, middle-class life, although he too was greatly influenced by his mother and her desire for her child to have artistic expression and commercial success.

After Dean's birth, the family moved to California, but

Dean's mother died when he was nine and his father sent him back to Indiana to be raised by an aunt and uncle. He lived with them for ten years, visited occasionally by his father, who had remarried.

Looking back on Dean's childhood and adolescence, no easy conclusions can be drawn to account for the eccentricities and neuroses that plagued Dean as a young adult. His life with his aunt and uncle was typical of a midwestern upbringing.

Dean won the Indiana State Contest of the National Forensic League, exhibiting his first interest in acting, and after graduating high school he drifted out to California to be closer to his father. But father and son never really communicated.

Dean started at Santa Monica City College to study law at his father's suggestion, but later abandoned the idea and transferred to UCLA. He dropped out after two years, leaving behind a reputation of being the

James Dean in *East of Eden*.

sloppiest of the sloppy in the blue jean-sweat shirt-dirty white shoes era.

He made television commercials and worked as an extra in films (*Fixed Bayonets* and *Sailor Beware*, 1951, *Has Anybody Seen My Gal*, 1952). Through roommate William Bast, he met actor James Whitmore, who suggested he go to New York and study at the Actors Studio.

Dean made a name for himself in New York in the Broadway production of *The Immoralist*, playing the young Arab servant and winning both the Donaldson and Antoinette Perry Awards. He had previously appeared on Broadway in 1952 in *See the Jaguar*, which starred Arthur Kennedy.

At this time, he also worked in the TV shows, "The Web," "Studio One," "Martin Kane, Private Eye," and "Suspense."

In the spring of 1954, Dean returned to Hollywood to star for Elia Kazan in *East of Eden*. Kazan had wanted Brando for the role, but he was unavailable. Even before the film's release, Dean became a star. Because he was the lead in a major Kazan picture (Kazan's first in CinemaScope). Dean received a big publicity buildup, and was heralded as "the new Brando."

Whatever publicity stunts Brando had been accused of pulling in the early 1950s, Dean now outdid him. Very publicity-conscious, he dressed sloppier than Brando, was even more tactless, and, with his all-night carousing, motorcycle riding and race-car driving, was considered even wilder than Brando. He became known as "the complete non-conformist" in Hollywood.

East of Eden was based on the 1952 John Steinbeck novel of the same title. Actually only a fragment of the novel was used in this screenplay by Paul Osborn, who had previously written six other "Eden" scripts, trying to cram the novel into a two-hour screenplay. The film, at the time of its release, represented a new relaxation in film censorship, since the Dean character's mother (Jo Van Fleet) was the town "Madam."

East of Eden turned out to be an excellent film, one of the rare cases where the publicity buildup was justified. Dean *was* an exciting new star. Both he and director Kazan received many superlative reviews. William K. Zinsser in the *New York Herald Tribune* said, "The characters in most Hollywood movies are fairly uncomplicated folk. They fall in and out of love at a moment's notice. They solve their problems with a punch on the jaw or a shot from the hip, and the director keeps things moving so fast that we don't have time to wonder why they behave as they do.

"Elia Kazan is a different kind of director. The people in his films are complex, and he wants to be very sure that you get to know and understand them. He takes his time. He lets his characters unfold slowly, and when

James Dean, Julie Harris in *East of Eden*.

Julie Harris received star billing in the Kazan film.

86

Dean, Jo Van Fleet in *East of Eden*.

they finally erupt into anger or violence, you know exactly why. This is the secret of *East of Eden*, Kazan's unbelievably sensitive movie. It is a poignant study of human emotions—and a distinguished picture."

From the 600-page, sprawling, three-generation novel, Kazan and writer Paul Osborn took only the final section, the part concerning the twin sons of Adam Trask— Aron, who inherited his father's kindness and conscience, and Cal, who inherited his mother's bad streak. Steinbeck intended this as a re-creation of the Abel and Cain legend, and the film preserved the novel's brooding tone.

The story concentrates on the inscrutable Cal, "and in this subtle role," said Zinsser, "a newcomer named James Dean gives a remarkable performance. He will inevitably be compared to Marlon Brando, for Kazan has stamped him with the same hesitant manner of speech, the same blind groping for love and security, that he gave Brando in *On the Waterfront*. But if the performances are akin, so are the roles, and to complain about the similarity would be quibbling."

Although Bosley Crowther congratulated Kazan on some aspects of the film, he was one of the few reviewers not taken with Dean's performance and was one of the quibblers. He said, "The director gets more into this picture with the scenery than with the characters.

"For the stubborn fact is that the people who move about in this film are not sufficiently well established to give point to the anguish through which they go, and the demonstrations of their torment are perceptibly stylized and grotesque. Especially is this true of James Dean in the role of the confused and cranky Cal. This young actor, who is here doing his first big screen stint, is a mass of histrionic gingerbread.

"He scuffs his feet, he whirls, he pouts, he sputters, he leans against walls, he rolls his eyes, he swallows his words, he ambles slack-kneed—all like Marlon Brando used to do. Never have we seen a performer so clearly follow another's style. Mr. Kazan should be spanked for permitting him to do such a sophomoric thing. Whatever there might be of reasonable torment in this youngster is buried beneath the clumsy display."

Zinsser totally disagreed and continued his praise: "Everything about Dean suggests the lonely, misunderstood nineteen-year-old. Even from a distance you know a lot about him by the way he walks—with his hands in his pockets and his head down, slinking like a dog waiting for a bone. When he talks, he stammers and pauses, uncertain of what he is trying to say. When he listens, he is full of restless energy—he stretches, he rolls on the ground, he chins himself on the porch railing, like a small boy impatient of his elders' chatter.

"When he suspects that his 'dead' mother is really alive, and hungrily begs his father (Raymond Massey) to

James Dean, Natalie Wood in *Rebel Without a Cause.* (1955)

James Dean fails to communicate with his parents, Jim Backus and Ann Doran, in *Rebel Without a Cause.*

The "rebel" characters existed in real life throughout the country.

James Dean involved in gang warfare, in *Rebel Without a Cause.*

It was Dean's second starring vehicle.

dredge up the facts of that unhappy marriage, he has the wounded look of an orphan trying to piece together the shabby facts of his heritage. And when he finally bursts in on his mother in the prosperous brothel she runs in Monterey, he has all the awkwardness of an adolescent who must ask a few tremendous questions and can only blurt them out crudely.

"Occasionally he smiles unaccountably, as if at some dark joke known only to him. 'He scares me,' his brother's girl Abra (Julie Harris) keeps saying, with reason. You sense the badness in him. But you also like him.

"How does Kazan know enough about human nature to mold such a performance? That is his genius. His technique is never obvious, but he pulls the moviegoer completely into the inner lives and thoughts of his characters."

Dean's publicized personal life and the image he created while the film was in production certainly helped the public accept this new screen rebel. Even though a successful movie star, he was projecting the image of a complex and troubled youth who felt unloved and was blindly lashing out at everything he thought was causing his unhappiness—hence his preoccupation with racing and courting death.

The role in *East of Eden*, and in *Rebel Without a Cause* as well, followed Dean's personal life in the sense that he had a strange, uncommunicative relationship with his own father.

Comparing Dean with Brando was the order of the day. *Look* said, "Because of a similarity in their acrobatic mannerisms, Dean inevitably will be compared to another Kazan actor, Marlon Brando. But nobody can deny Dean's personal achievement in making his difficult role understandable and fascinating." *Look* also said, *East of Eden* is so sharply different from other current films that it is bound to be talked about—pro and con—for months to come."

While Dean's acting style was certainly derivative of the Clift-Brando school, it worked in his case because he was so physically unlike either of them.

In discussing *East of Eden*, Brando at the time was quoted as saying, "Jim and I worked together at Actors Studio in New York, and I have great respect for his talent. However, in that film, Mr. Dean appears to be wearing my last year's wardrobe and using my last year's talent."

It was reported that Dean and Brando used the same psychoanalyst and this further cemented the theory that Dean was a carbon copy of Brando. Dean's retort was, "I have my own personal rebellion and don't have to rely on Brando's."

Kate Cameron, in the *New York Daily News*, said: "While everyone else who's seen him compared him to Marlon Brando, Kazan makes no such comparison. To him, Dean is a fine young actor whose personality and talent are strictly his own.

"But those who have seen previews of the new film say that if you close your eyes while Dean is speaking, you'll swear you are listening to Brando, and they are wondering just how much of Brando is really Kazan."

In any case, Dean's own talents were extraordinary. Riding high on *East of Eden's* success, Dean's personal life continued to become more flamboyant. He had a much-publicized romance with Pier Angeli, considered by many to be "the one great love of his life." After splitting with her he went to work in *Rebel Without a Cause* and began an affair with a little-known German starlet, Ursula Andress.

Dean had been quoted as saying, "I think there's only one true form of greatness for a man. If a man can bridge the gap between life and death—I mean, if he can live on after he's dead—then maybe he was a great man. . . . To me, the only success, the only greatness . . . is in immortality."

In September, 1955, after finishing *Rebel Without a Cause* and *Giant*, he turned his attention from motorcycle racing to sports cars. On September 30, at the age of twenty-four, he was killed in an automobile accident in the California desert and the Dean legend began. Warner Bros. released *Rebel Without a Cause* one month after Dean's death. The James Dean cult sprang up.

Rebel was a box-office hit, although surprisingly it did not receive unanimous critical raves. The *New York Herald Tribune* critic Zinsser said, "The movie is written and acted so ineptly, directed so sluggishly, that all names but one will be omitted here. The exception is Dean, the gifted young actor who was killed last month. His rare talent and appealing personality even shine through this turgid melodrama." But Bosley Crowther in *The New York Times* said, "It is a violent, brutal and disturbing picture of modern teenagers. Young people neglected by their parents or given no understanding and moral support by fathers and mothers who are themselves unable to achieve balance and security in their homes are the bristling heroes and heroines of this excessively graphic exercise. Like *Blackboard Jungle* before it, it is a picture to make the hair stand on end."

The film was directed by Nicholas Ray, and is still considered his best film. Ray was the assistant director to Elia Kazan on the 1945 film, *A Tree Grows in Brooklyn*, and made his impressive directorial debut at thirty-six with *They Live by Night* (1947). Among his next half-dozen films was a small, now forgotten Humphrey Bogart vehicle, *In a Lonely Place*, in which Bogart was the ultimate anti-hero. Gloria Grahame (later Mrs. Ray) played a hardbitten heroic heroine.

After several programmers in the early 1950s, Ray hit his stride with *Rebel Without a Cause*. Although the

Sal Mineo.
Mineo received
co-star billing in
Rebel Without a Cause
and enjoyed a brief popularity.

Mineo was a
juvenile delinquent in
Crime in the Streets,
Don Siegel's film which starred
James Whitmore and John Cassavetes. Mineo
had a short-lived career as a sort of 1950s Dead End Kid.

screenplay by Stewart Stern (adapted by Irving Schulman from a story by Ray himself) was a bit weak in characterization, it was generally effective and pointed to the lack of communication between youngsters and their parents that would eventually widen into the "generation gap."

Dean once again played a troubled youth. Again he was struggling to communicate with an unfeeling father. As a new student in a high school in Los Angeles, Dean encounters violence and meets two other misunderstood teenagers, portrayed by Natalie Wood and Sal Mineo.

He meets these two in jail, where he has been taken on a drunk and disorderly charge. Dean and Natalie have an immediate rapport, and Mineo warns them against Natalie's boyfriend, Buzz. Buzz and his gang slash the tires of Dean's car and a fight ensues. The boys decide to settle their differences by having a "chicken run." Each will drive a stolen car towards a precipice and the first to jump before the car lunges over will be "chicken." Dean's parents, portrayed by Jim Backus and Ann Doran, do nothing to stop the chicken run, and with Natalie as timekeeper the run goes off on schedule. Dean, whose character is called Jim in the story, leaps to safety before his car goes over the cliff. But Buzz

goes down with his car. Mineo, a lost and hero-searching lad, has made Dean his hero. And Buzz' gang, in retaliation for Buzz's death, brutally beats Mineo in a compelling scene in an empty swimming pool. Mineo manages to warn Dean that he is next, and in the process Mineo, pursued by parents and police, panics and is killed by a policeman's bullet. Crowther discussed "a wistful and truly poignant stretch wherein Mr. Dean and Miss Wood as lonely exiles from their own homes try to pretend they are happy grown-ups in an old mansion. There are some excruciating flashes of accuracy and truth in this film."

Crowther then went on to say he wished the young actors in the film, including Mr. Dean, were not so intent on imitating Marlon Brando.

Dean had the uncanny ability to inspire audience identification in the young. In the 1950s, the two basic ways that youth could rebel seemed to be through acts of violence and delinquency *(The Blackboard Jungle* vividly described that situation) and through gathering, herd-like, into groups and being directed by a group leader. Although this last would sometimes lead to unlawful acts, the group's prime concern was not violence and unlawfulness but a search for security and mass identification. Not unlike college fraternities, but on a more general and less organized level, these groups or clubs of youths would have special jackets, sweaters, emblems, meeting places, etc.

Hence, the youth of the fifties found *Rebel Without a Cause* and its rebel hero, off-screen as well as on-screen, easy to identify with.

Dean had an astonishing hold on the adolescent imagination; he brought authority to the role of the "crazy, mixed-up kid." As they had done with Brando and Clift before, America's youth was choosing a disturbed man to represent their suffering, rather than a Greek hero.

Warners did not release *Giant* until October, 1956, thirteen months after Dean's death. By that time, the Dean cult was in full flower. Ironically, his last film did not present him as a rebel hero, but as a surly ranch hand who becomes an oil baron. In the latter part of the film, he was in character makeup, with moustache, dark glasses and a dissipated look. However, as *New York Herald Tribune* critic Herb Kupferberger noted, "His earlier depiction of the amoral, reckless, animal-like young ranch hand will not only excite his admirers to frenzy, it will make the most sedate onlooker under-stand why the James Dean cult ever came into existence."

Giant garnered great reviews. Elizabeth Taylor and Rock Hudson were discussed favorably, but the critics' superlatives were bestowed upon James Dean in the role of Jett Rink. *The New York Times* said, "It is the late James Dean who makes [his] malignant role . . . the most tangy and corrosive in the film. Mr. Dean plays this curious villain with a stylized spookiness—a sly sort of off-beat languor and slur of language—that concentrates spite. This is a haunting capstone to the brief career of Mr. Dean."

"Jett's introversion and resentment are conveyed in the arresting terms of another Dean-age rebel," said the *Christian Science Monitor*.

Even *Time*, seldom generous with its praise of films and performances, admitted, "James Dean, who was killed in a sports-car crash two weeks after his last scene in *Giant* was shot, in this film clearly shows for the first (and fatefully the last) time what his admirers always said he had: a streak of genius. He has caught the Texas accent to nasal perfection, and mastered the lock-hipped, high-heeled stagger of the wrangler, and the wry little jerks and smirks, tics and twitches, grunts and giggles that make up most of the language of a man

James Dean becomes a successful oil baron in *Giant*.

Rock Hudson, James Dean in *Giant*.

James Dean, Elizabeth Taylor in *Giant*,
with Dean in crucifixion pose.

James Dean drills for oil in *Giant*.

who talks to himself a good deal more than he does to anyone else. In one scene, indeed, in a long, drunken mumble with actress Carroll Baker in an empty cocktail lounge, Dean is able to press an amazing array of subtleties into the mood of the moment, to achieve what is certainly the finest piece of atmospheric acting seen on screen since Marlon Brando and Rod Steiger did their 'brother scene' in *On the Waterfront*."

In addition to Taylor, Hudson, Dean and Baker, the film co-starred Jane Withers, Chill Wills, Mercedes McCambridge, Sal Mineo and a newcomer, Dennis Hopper. But the real star of *Giant* was its director, George Stevens, who also produced the film, with Henry Ginzberg. Fred Guiol and Ivan Moffatt wrote the screenplay, based on the novel by Edna Ferber. *Variety* correctly predicted that *Giant* would be "box-office dynamite."

Dean had signed a new contract with Warners during the shooting of *Rebel Without a Cause*, calling for nine films over a six-year period. He completed only *Giant*. In October, 1957, two years after his death and with a flourishing cult following to support it, Warner Bros. released *The James Dean Story*, a feature-length documentary, to capitalize on the legend. This was a sketchy compilation, including still photographs from school and family albums, film, letters, interviews with family and friends who knew him when he was a boy and a young man. Martin Gabel narrated the film, which had a featured song, "Let Me Be Loved," sung by Tommy Sands. Several points were illuminated in the film. Dean had a great interest in drawing and modeling. He loathed all forms of violence. He had a deep love for the countryside. One point that may have been a slight surprise to his fans was that he habitually wore glasses, which may have accounted for that distant searching look in his eyes when he was acting.

The Dean legend was international, and the venerable London *Times* reviewed the documentary on Dean's life. "When a film goes by the title of the So-and-So Story," said *The Times*, "the odds are that it will turn out to be a biography so filled with sentimental fancy that any connection with the truth will be miraculous. *The James Dean Story*, produced and directed by Mr. G. W. George and Robert Altman, is not quite like that. It can, indeed, almost claim to be regarded as a documentary, since it relies to a great extent on documentary facts, on photographs, on letters, on interviews with relatives and others who knew Dean as a child, as a boy, and during the short time he achieved fame, a garland briefer than a girl's, before his fatal motor accident on September 30, 1955." *The Times* also said that the film drew a portrait of Dean as "A lonely young man, haunted by insecurity, longing for affection yet thrusting it away from him, gifted yet suspecting his gifts, ambitious yet preferring to live like a tramp, in love, like T. E. Lawrence, with speed, and hugging a surly manner around him like a protecting cloak."

If there was any doubt, the film proved that, though young and having made only three films, James Dean was a screen legend of the first magnitude. It was an intimate portrait that painted Dean as the idol of his contemporaries because he expressed a sense of rebellion combined with a desperate need for affection, which all youth felt, but was unable to express.

Bosley Crowther called the film, "An effective contribution to the perpetuation of the Legend."

In addition to the film, many books sprang up about Dean, and were eagerly devoured by the Dean cultists. William Bast, Dean's former roommate and later a publicist at Warner Bros., published a book about Dean, and other books were published in French and German. Perhaps the most tasteless book capitalizing on Dean's untimely death was Walter Ross' novel, *The Immortal*, published by Simon & Schuster. Ross contended, "This story is not about any real people, alive or dead." These few words of denial took up an entire page in the book, as if that would make them more believable.

The Immortal is about John Preston, a middle west foster child, furtive and unpredictable, who becomes a successful actor in films. He is attractive to men and women of all ages. He is sometimes a dreadful person, sometimes charming. His cultists pretend that he still lives.

After Dean's death, spiritualists and other people believing in the supernatural contended that they could communicate with him. Many writers began saying that the Dean legend had taken an unhealthy turn, with this emphasis on the supernatural and his image as a frustrated, mixed-up youth advocating rebellion.

His followers had lost sight of him as an actor and thought of him as a martyr for uncommunicative youth. In 1957 the James Dean Memorial Foundation was set up, to "translate the force of his legend into constructive channels." They arranged for a James Dean Theatre School to be conducted in Fairmont, Indiana, Dean's home town, under the auspices of Earlham College. *Variety* later reported, however, that after eighteen months of operation, the James Dean Foundation collapsed owing to lack of funds.

James Dean's legend had a see-saw existence for the next fifteen years. Whenever people thought it had completely died, something would pop up—a series of articles in 1960, a series of posters in 1964, a poem in the *Village Voice* in 1966, a two-page poster spread in the *New York Daily News* in 1967.

Curiosity seekers have chipped away parts of the headstone at Dean's grave. Articles have been written about people who are still avid James Dean fans fifteen years after his death, collecting such intimate objects as the teddy bear he used in *Rebel Without a Cause*. The Laurence Hutton Collection, at Princeton University, includes a life mask of Dean, along with masks of Beethoven, Keats and other immortals.

Because of his untimely death, Dean did not have an opportunity to build a following over the years. Left unanswered is the question of whether or not Dean could have broken out of the rebel mold. The hard-core Dean cultists are basically of his generation. Today's youth have their own rebel heroes. And when Dean died, a generation not only mourned him, but in fact mourned its own demise.

In 1961, *East of Eden* was re-issued in Europe. In London, the *Sunday Times* said, "When *East of Eden* appeared, it was fashionable to say that Dean tried to imitate Brando. Well, if he tried he certainly didn't succeed, and in the result the only resemblance I can see is in the use of the broken, half-masticated phrase.

"Brando is all power: power sometimes pinioned, or trapped, or degraded, but still power. James Dean was sentenced by physique to stand for defenselessness; and some instinct, far more than the actor's technique, taught him how to suggest, behind the mask of rebelliousness, a different being, shrinking, fragile, not quite fully grown. As long as he stuck to that he had no equal; and look-

ing again at this first film I am astounded by his performance. It is even better than I had thought: more truly anguished, more delicately poised between the awkward, sulky scapegoat and the young creature exploding with love. It gives heart and center to the film, it breathes life into Kazan's melodramatics." The paper continued, "Perhaps as an actor he was lucky to die half-tried, before he could be forced out of his adolescent's shell. In *East of Eden,* at any rate, his wistful image is undisturbed."

To his generation, and for all film historians, Dean will always represent the ultimate rebel, the symbol of self-pitying youth, rebelling against the insecurity and loneliness in his own soul.

Dean aged convincingly as Jett Rink in the George Stevens film.

6
The Rebel Hero in Transition: The Heel as Hero

During the next ten years, the rebel hero of the screen underwent a fantastic transition. The youth of America did not have one particular actor or screen character who captured their imagination as Dean had. From 1957 through 1967, American films produced three major new stars who played both rebel heroes and anti-heroes as well as traditional heroes: Paul Newman, Steve McQueen and Warren Beatty. In addition, established rebels like Marlon Brando, Montgomery Clift and Frank Sinatra, checkered their careers with a variety of characterizations.

Although there was no studio-concentrated effort to manufacture a new rebel, as Warner's had engineered the careers of Garfield and Dean, films with leading characters possessing rebel hero qualities sporadically appeared.

John Garfield had purchased a property, *The Man With the Golden Arm*, in 1950. It was about drug addiction, then a taboo subject for filmization. Garfield had bought the National Book Award-winning novel by Nelson Algren, who had also written a screenplay. But, as Garfield said, in 1951, "The Breen office nixed it. Can't show drug addiction, so I can't make it, I can't defy the Breen office. But I love it [the script]. I love it so much it just gives me pleasure to own it."

Paul Newman (with director Robert Rossen).

Steve McQueen (with James Coburn and Robert Vaughan). Newman, Beatty and McQueen were destined to become the top rebel stars of the sixties.

Warren Beatty.

By 1956, several major films had been released without the production code seal. Other films had already handled previously taboo subjects (Detective Story, Otto Preminger's The Moon Is Blue). Producer-director Preminger acquired the rights to The Man With the Golden Arm. With a new screenplay written by Walter Newman and Lewis Meltzer, the role Garfield had coveted so highly went to Frank Sinatra.

Preminger cast Sinatra in the part, although he could have as easily cast Marlon Brando. The director has said, "When I had about thirty or forty pages of the script ready, I gave one copy to Sinatra's agent and one to Brando's agent, just to give them an idea of what the picture was about. I got a call the next day from Sinatra's agent, who said, 'He likes it very much.' I said, 'All right, I'll send him the rest of the script as soon as I have it.' He said, 'No, he wants to do it without reading the rest of the script.' "

Preminger thus cast Sinatra rather than Brando simply because the actor had come to a quick decision. He was not disappointed with his choice, however, and has said, "It was a wonderful experience. I've never enjoyed working with anyone more than Sinatra."

The character of Frankie Machine was certainly not the rebel hero of the Clift-Brando-Dean school. In fact, he was not a hero at all, but a weak man caught up in drug addiction. But the character represented a man who, in his rebellion against what fate had dealt him, turned to drugs—not being able to cope with a slum environment existence, a self-centered, nagging wife, and a guilty conscience because he thinks he crippled her in an automobile accident. As the film opens, he is returning from being cured of drug addiction at a Federal hospital.

He is now faced with inner conflicts—he loves a woman other than his wife and he wants to find a job as a drummer so he needn't go back to being a gambler. (The "Golden Arm" of the title refers to the fact that Frankie is an expert dealer, who can control a card game with instinctive skill.) And he is confronted with outer conflicts—returning to the slum environment and the neighborhood pusher.

Although Sinatra's performance won rave reviews and an Academy Award nomination, it was the subject matter of the film and the Motion Picture Association of America's refusal to grant the film a seal which made all the headlines.

United Artists' original agreement with Preminger was a conditional one concerning distribution of the film. But after seeing the finished product, they announced that they would go ahead and distribute the film with or without a seal.

Arthur Knight in Saturday Review said, "The film is definitely worth talking about, even cheering about. It is a bold, forthright, harrowing study of an addict and how he got that way. And, just as excerpts from *Dr. Ehrlich's Magic Bullet* are now used regularly in our schools as part of sex-education programs, it is not at all inconceivable that a future generation will learn something of the evils of narcotics through sequences from this extraordinary film.... Frankie Machine is no admirable character, no titan laid low by tragedy. In fact, the traditional concepts of tragedy have no place in this story. As with so much of contemporary fiction, its central character is a hero in name only—a weak, insignificant little man with a shabby code of ethics and a golden arm at poker. But even without admiring him one can feel for him, recognizing the honest loyalty he has for the neurotic wife he crippled in an auto accident, his touching relationship with the B-girl, his small pride at dealing an honest game. And with that feeling one watches with horror as he follows the 'pusher' to take his first fix 'for the last time,' and shares his degradation when his pitiful shred of honor is subordinated to his craving for drugs and he consents to deal a crooked hand. It is the tragedy of the small soul, but drawn with a terrifying intensity.''

By the end of the film, Kim Novak, although a B-girl and a long way from Priscilla Lane, is nonetheless portraying a heroic heroine who helps the hero back onto the right track, in this case kicking the habit once again.

Films began exploring these heretofore taboo subjects because the industry was facing fierce competition from television.

In the thirties and forties the stage had served as the training ground for film stars. In the fifties and sixties television became an equally important training ground for actors. In 1952, a young actor from Cleveland, with only summer stock experience, came to New York and worked in video dramas such as ''The Web,'' ''You Are There,'' and ''Danger,'' before landing a role in William Inge's play, *Picnic*. He had tried out for the leading role, the heel, Hal Carter, but he was cast as the college boy, Alan Seymour. When *Picnic* opened on February 19, 1953, Brooks Atkinson of *The New York Times* said, ''Paul Newman, as a college lad infatuated with pretty faces ... [helps] to bring to life all the cross-currents of Mr. Inge's sensitive writing.''

Warner Bros., the studio famous for discovering rebel heroes, saw Newman's potential and signed him to a long-term contract, and the actor left the cast of *Picnic* before it went on its national tour.

But Warners never used Newman in a rebel hero role. In fact, they never cast him in a blockbuster movie. He was put into *The Silver Chalice*, a critical and financial disaster, described by Newman as ''the worst motion picture filmed during the fifties. They lent him to MGM for *The Rack*, in which he played a Korean war veteran

The Man With the Golden Arm had originally been bought by John Garfield at a time when the production code office wouldn't permit him to film it.

Kim Novak, as the good girl, albeit ''B'' girl, and Sinatra in *The Man With the Golden Arm*.

Sinatra as the dealer exposed at cheating, in *The Man With the Golden Arm*.

on trial for collaboration. Some elements of what Newman would later project on screen as the decade's ultimate rebel-anti-hero came through when he played this part of a boy-man caught in the trap of war.

After these two films, Newman returned to Broadway to appear as a psychotic gunman in Joseph Hayes' play, *The Desperate Hours*. He also returned to televesion late in 1955, and portrayed a 55-year-old fighter in *The Battler*, a television script based on an Ernest Hemingway short story.

Newman portrayed what might be considered his first rebel hero screen role in 1957, in MGM's *Somebody Up There Likes Me*. It was a rather realistic screen biography of the fighter Rocky Graziano, depicting his rise from the slums to become middleweight boxing champion of the world.

"In this asserted biography of Rocky Graziano," wrote Bosley Crowther, "who rose from reform school and penitentiary to the middleweight championship of the world, the prize ring is highly recommended as a fine place for a tough to vent his spleen and gain for himself not only money but also public applause and respect."

In discussing the heroic heroine, Crowther continued, "Now that the means of salvation (fighting) has been happily found, the remaining job of direction is left to a fine, devoted girl. She is presented in the person of lovely Pier Angeli, who does as much for the hero—and for the picture—as does somebody up there. When romance and sentiment take over, the story of the hoodlum is done.

"Let it be said of Mr. Newman that he plays the role of Graziano well, making the pug and Marlon Brando almost indistinguishable. He is funny, tough and pathetic in that slouching, rolling, smirking Brando style, but with a quite apparent simulation of the mannerisms of the former middleweight champ."

Newman, like Brando, influenced by the Actors Studio method, studied his characters carefully. He spent two weeks with Graziano observing his daily regimen.

After a series of varied roles, as a son-of-a-bitch in *The Helen Morgan Story*, a somewhat unconventional hero (bordering on anti-hero) in *Until They Sail*, and as Billy the Kid in Arthur Penn's stylistic *The Left-Handed Gun*, Newman appeared as Ben Quick in *The Long Hot Summer*, a 20th Century-Fox film released in 1958.

By that time Newman had divorced his first wife, Jackie Witte, with whom he had three children, and married actress Joanne Woodward, whom he met while she understudied in *Picnic*. Newman and Woodward (she had won the Best Actress Oscar in 1957 for *Three Faces of Eve*) co-starred in *The Long Hot Summer*, an adaptation of several William Faulkner short stories and his novel *The Hamlet*. Almost a throwback to the Garfield character of the thirties and forties, as Ben Quick

Newcomer to Hollywood Paul Newman, photographed with established star Grace Kelly.

Newman triumphs as Rocky Graziano in *Somebody Up There Likes Me*. James Dean was originally set for this role, as well as the role of Billy the Kid, in MGM's *The Left-Handed Gun*. Both parts went to Newman.

100

Newman was a vocal, dissatisfied nonconformist who knew exactly what the heroine wanted and told her so.

"Paul Newman is best as the roughneck who moves in with a thinly veiled sneer to knock down the younger generation and make himself the inheritor of the old man," said *The New York Times*. "He has within his plowhand figure and behind his hard blue eyes the deep and ugly deceptions of a neo-Huey Long. He could, if the script would let him, develop a classic character."

That same year, the two leading rebel heroes of the decade, Clift and Brando, were cast in the same film. Along with Dean Martin, they starred in the film version of Irwin Shaw's highly successful novel, *The Young Lions*.

Brando and Clift were at odds during production over interpretation of roles. Brando played a Nazi officer, and succeeded in making him a sensitive, sympathetic character. He had bleached his hair blond for the role, and critics said he resorted to Kowalski for characterization. Clift portrayed a Jewish-American GI, who was a martyr in the story. Clift was annoyed with Brando, since he was trying to turn his Nazi character into a martyr. At the end of the picture, when the Nazi officer was shot

and staggered down a hill, Brando suggested that he fall across a heap of barbed wire, arms outstretched. Clift threatened to walk off the set, and an onlooker noted, "When Clift's around, there's only room for one Jesus Christ."

Many critics reported that the most noticeable of changes in the transition from novel to screen was the character of the young Nazi. In Irwin Shaw's book this young warrior was presented as a fairly decent ski instructor who, under the hammering of Naziism and war, was molded into a monster. But in the film version, this significantly unregenerate Nazi was changed into a very nice young man who never embraced Naziism with any zeal. He regards war with disgust and sadness and is finally killed when roughly disillusioned and sick to death of it all. *The New York Times* said, "As played by Marlon Brando, with his hair dyed a shiny cornsilk blond and his voice affecting a German accent reminiscent of Weber and Fields, this fellow is sensitive and attractive. He evokes complete sympathy. He has the gentleness of one of those nice young Germans in the memorable *All Quiet on the Western Front*. Indeed, there is much

Newman, Pier Angeli as his "good girl" wife in *Somebody Up There Likes Me*.

Clift in *Indiscretion of an American Wife,* a Selznick picture co-starring Mrs. Selznick (Jennifer Jones) and directed by Vittorio de Sica.

Clift, Elizabeth Taylor in *Raintree County,* in which he received top billing. "Indiscretion" and "Raintree" were two of his films before returning to rebel roles.

about *The Young Lions* that is mindful of that film. It is not so much anti-Nazi as it is vaguely and loosely antiwar."

Paul V. Beckley in the *New York Herald Tribune* agreed. "Brando's role has been idealized. He is a Diestl who 'thinks of peace a thousand times a day,' who risks courtmartial to protest the mistreating of a French prisoner, who refuses in combat a direct order to shoot a wounded prisoner. This toning down of Shaw's mean, arrogant, cruel and brutish killer has made it a less striking characterization than it otherwise would have been."

But Beckley thought, "Clift on the other hand is superb in his inarticulate anguish as he talks with his girl's father, who has never met a Jew. He is no less so in the trying and brutal scenes in the training camp. Miss (Hope) Lange, too, gives a tender performance as his betrothed. Dean Martin, playing his first serious character role, does very well as the charming actor with a surface callousness."

But the *Times* noted, "As it happens, Mr. Brando makes the German much more vital and interesting than Montgomery Clift and Dean Martin make the Americans. Mr. Clift is strangely hollow and lackluster as the sensitive Jew. He acts throughout the picture as if he were in a glassy-eyed daze. And Mr. Martin plays a Broadway showman pulled into the army against his will, as if he was lonesome for Jerry Lewis and didn't know exactly what to do."

The Young Lions was Clift's first film after *Raintree County,* and only his third since *From Here to Eternity.* But it had been five years since the latter film, and during production of *Raintree County,* Clift had a nearly fatal automobile accident, which drastically changed his

physical appearance. This change, accompanied by his seeming inability to cope with personal problems, vanity about his age and looks, and drinking, severely hampered his future career in films.

The Young Lions represented a return to the rebel character for Brando, who had tried non-rebel roles (*Desiree,* 1954; *Guys and Dolls,* 1955; *Teahouse of the August Moon,* 1956; *Sayonara,* 1957). It was a big hit, and he followed it up with another rebel character, Val Xavier in Tennessee Williams' *The Fugitive Kind,* based on Williams' play *Orpheus Descending.*

This had been Williams' first full-length play, and it had always been a critical and commercial disaster. But he kept re-writing and reviving it. Even under Sidney Lumet's direction and with a stellar cast headed by Brando, tempestuous Anna Magnani, and intense Joanne Woodward, success still eluded the 1960 film version.

Brando portrayed a vagabond. The character was rebeling against conformity and the narrowmindedness of a symbolic small Southern town. In fact, the film might even be considered a forerunner to *Easy Rider,* with Brando representing the hippie, beat, bohemian character, and Victor Jory the redneck Southerner.

Archer Winsten seemed to be speaking for most critics when he said, "Old man Marlon plays it cool all the time, now holding his head high and looking down like a Buddha, then putting his head down and looking upward and off to one side while he tries to think of what to say. It's no accident that women seem to think of him as standing at stud.

"The Brando, Woodward and Magnani stints are all emotionally magnificent in their highly individual ways. Maureen Stapleton and Victor Jory are also notable.

There is nothing about production, performances, or direction that fails to strike one as picture-making in the best, big style. Only the play itself seems questionable, though that must seem a traitorous sentiment to those who idolize Williams in all of his bizarre phases."

Producer Sam Spiegel then wanted Brando for *Lawrence of Arabia*, but Brando spent most of 1960 writing and directing his own production for Paramount, *One Eyed Jacks*, a project that mushroomed from a modestly budgeted Western into a $6 million spectacular. (Originally Stanley Kubrick began directing the film, which was budgeted at $1.8 million.)

It was Brando's first and last directorial attempt to date. Although the film was a financial disaster because of its huge cost, it received wide critical acclaim. Millions went to see it and obviously relished Brando in his classic rebel mold. Once again, like the character of Kowalski in "Streetcar," he portrayed a vulgar ruffian possessing sensitivity. It was Brando's first Western, and he selected an unknown Mexican actress, Pina Pellicer, for the role of the good girl who helps the rebel hero towards reformation. Brando hoped the role would serve to make Miss Pellicer a star, as Eva Marie Saint had become after *On the Waterfront*.

Concerning the film, Bosley Crowther remarked, "What is extraordinary about it is that it proceeds in two contrasting styles. One is hard and realistic; the other is romantic and lush. All the way through it runs a jangle of artistic ambivalence. It is as if it had been directed jointly by John Huston and Raoul Walsh."

The title refers to the one-sidedness of the face man reveals to the world, the implication being that good men have a bad side to their face, the bad a good one.

In the film, Brando seduces the stepdaughter of his enemy then ultimately realizes his love for her and wants to forsake his life of crime to marry her. The hero is portrayed as patient and eventually reasonable. The villains, presented as noisy and arrogant, are never reasonable. Critics thought Brando the director "showed promise."

The *New York Post*'s Archer Winsten commented, "In the history of movie acting there has been no performer who could maintain a pensive silence quite as effectively as Marlon Brando, and director Marlon Brando knows this, so he gives the actor his head, as it were, plus situation, background and lighting, and what you get is invariably a damned tense moment."

Jokes had arisen in Hollywood that a sure way to get Brando to agree to star in a film was to promise him a scene where he gets severely beaten, and *One Eyed Jacks* was one of his most gory films up to that time. In one scene, Malden smashes Brando's hand to raw meat.

In Brando's original version, the leading lady was killed. But he was persuaded to change this since it was

Montgomery Clift, Dean Martin in *The Young Lions*. It was Clift's return to a rebel hero-type role.

Hope Lange, Clift in *The Young Lions*.

Brando, May Britt in *The Young Lions*. He was a sympathetic Nazi with rebel hero overtones.

Maximilian Schell, then relatively unknown, and Brando in *The Young Lions*.

too downbeat. His version of the film ran over five hours. Paramount pared it down considerably for general distribution, and from that point on Brando, extremely unhappy with the film, said "it was not an artistic success." He even called it a "potboiler."

Brando's next excursion into filmmaking was MGM's much publicized remake of *Mutiny on the Bounty*. During the production of this film, Marlon's off-screen rebel image surpassed any character he could possibly portray in films and for a new generation of moviegoers the off-screen rebel Marlon was forever meshed with his on-screen characters. The "fantastic" budget of *One Eyed Jacks* became petty cash compared to the epic $27 million negative cost of *Mutiny on the Bounty*.

According to then 66-year-old director Lewis Milestone, who was called in to replace the original director, Carol Reed, who had resigned, "This picture should have been called *The Mutiny of Marlon Brando*."

Why they decided to remake this film (the original could have been re-released) is still a question. Remaking *Imitation of Life*, or other stories that can indeed be updated, or remaking *Ben Hur* or *The Ten Commandments* from silent into sound films is justifiable. The original *Mutiny on the Bounty* had excellent performances by Clark Gable, Charles Laughton, and Franchot Tone, a cohesive script, and scope, even though on small screen and in black and white. Most of these ingredients were lacking in the wide-screen Technicolor star-studded 1963 version.

The production was chaos from the beginning. The ship, the *Bounty*, was not constructed in time for the start of production. There was no complete shooting

script. Writers were changed in midstream. Brando decided that instead of Fletcher Christian he should play another character, Seaman John Adams, the lone survivor of the mutiny. This idea was vetoed. By this time, the film, being shot on location, encountered the Tahitian rainy season. When Milestone replaced Carol Reed, Brando and he were immediately in conflict. Milestone accused the actor of wearing earplugs so he couldn't hear the director or the other actors.

While Brando was on the set every day, and scenes were shot, little footage was usable. His relationship with producer Aaron Rosenberg became as strained as with Milestone. It is reported that after several endings for the film were shot and discarded, the final ending was shot on an MGM sound stage in Hollywood, with Brando actually directing and Milestone sitting in his dressing room reading magazines.

Concerning the film, Brando has said that the costs that piled up in the filming of *Mutiny on the Bounty* were the result of poor executive operations. "The reason for all the big failures is the same," he said. "No script." He said that when that happens the star of the film becomes the target of the executives "trying to cover their own tracks . . . executives most of whom have gone into the fog and smog of LA." Carol Reed, the director who had first been engaged to put *Mutiny on the Bounty* on the screen, resigned from the job, and Brando says that he himself had been asked several times to take over the direction of the film before Milestone was named as the replacement.

"An actor is a product," continued Brando," like Ford cars or Florsheim shoes. He's a useful product that is resold many times for social purposes; then there's the money, and he's just generally exploited the way any other piece of merchandise is. And whenever it was that the press realized that the antics or the tragedies or the general activities of actors was a useful commodity, then I think the relations between them took a new turn.

"Actually, you see, it's not the press. It's the public, because that's what they want to read."

Brando maintained, "As long as there's a market for the scandal item there will be people to hawk it. And as long as there are actors who want to be exploited, it'll always be the same.

"But," he continued, "over the years, it hasn't mattered much because people see enough lies on television and enough lies in the newspapers to know that policy dictates the nature of the information to such an extent that they don't believe what they read, even though they accept it as a possibility. I find one phrase that comes up so often—'What's he really like?'— whether they're talking about Frank Sinatra or Mickey Rooney. . . . And there's something else, it's closer to embarrassment than anything else. As soon as you be-

Some non-rebel roles for Brando:

Always excellent at makeup, Brando portrayed the enterprising Okinawan houseboy in *Teahouse of the August Moon,* with Paul Ford and Glenn Ford.

Brando, Red Buttons and Miyoshi Umeki in *Sayonara.*

Desiree, with Jean Simmons. Brando disliked the film.

105

The two emotional powerhouses in *The Fugitive Kind*.

come an actor, people start asking you questions about politics, astrology, archeology, and birth control. And what's funnier, you start giving opinions."

Everyone's worst fears that the film wouldn't recoup its costs were realized, despite surprisingly good reviews. The film was one of MGM's biggest financial disasters.

Brando's off-screen rebel image was at its zenith. In addition to all the negative publicity about the film, his personal life continued to make headlines.

Critics have claimed that in his early career his rebellious image was mainly publicity-oriented, and they are probably right. Brando has a zany sense of humor and he revelled in giving the press misinformation about his personal life.

In the early fifties, he had a much-publicized romance and engagement to Josanne Marianna-Berenger, the daughter of a French fisherman. There was also his on-again off-again romance with actress Rita Moreno, who at one time attempted suicide because of their relationship. (However, their tempestuous affair mellowed into a genuine, lasting friendship.)

Brando had also been linked romantically with France Nuyen, the Eurasian star of Broadway's *The World of Suzie Wong*. It is reported that because of her relation-

Brando, Magnani and Joanne Woodward in *The Fugitive Kind*.

The vigilantes take Brando in *The Fugitive Kind*, film version of Tennessee Williams' *Orpheus Descending*.

Brando, Pina Pellicer in *One Eyed Jacks*. He hoped the picture would make her a star, as *Waterfront* had done for Eva Marie Saint.

Katy Jurado, Brando, Karl Malden in *One Eyed Jacks*. Again Malden provided excellent support.

Brando in *One Eyed Jacks*.
It was never a financial success but only because of its high production cost; a large audience turned out to see it.

ship with Brando she became unable to make the film version of *Suzie,* and was replaced by Nancy Kwan.

Over the years, Brando has had an obvious penchant for exotic women. His first marriage was in 1957, to Anna Kashfi, seemingly an exotic Eurasian from New Dehli, although she turned out to be Joan O'Callahan, more Irish than Indian. With Miss Kashfi, Brando has a son, Christian Devi. Their marriage was a short one, followed by years of court battles and custody fights over the child. After divorcing Miss Kashfi in 1960 (they had been separated in 1958), Brando married his long-time friend, Mexican actress Movita. A few months after the marriage, Movita gave birth to Brando's second son, Miko.

During the filming of *Mutiny on the Bounty*, Brando had a third son, Tehotu, with his co-star, Tahitian beauty Tarita. (In February, 1970, Tarita gave birth to Brando's first daughter, also called Tarita.) While his private life remains a mystery, further confused by the fact that Brando himself gives out conflicting reports regarding his marriages and children, it is a fact that he is a devoted father. He makes an attempt to see all of his children regularly, and to keep them in touch with each other.

After *Mutiny on the Bounty*, Brando played no more rebel roles. But his price remained in the million-dollar category, despite diminishing returns for Brando pictures at the box office.

He gave a good performance in *The Ugly American* (1963), a broad but effective one in *Bedtime Story* (1964), his first attempt at sophisticated comedy, and a muddled performance in *Morituri* (1965). Even though he was beaten up severely in scenes for *The Chase* (1966) and

Brando directing Malden.

Gable and Movita

Brando and Tarita

Gable and Laughton (who got top billing)

Brando and Trevor Howard

Richard Harris in *Mutiny on the Bounty*. He hated working with Brando.

The Appaloosa (1966), both were critical and commercial disappointments. His second attempt at sophisticated comedy, Charles Chaplin's 1967 film *The Countess from Hong Kong* was widely publicized, but critics were expecting a comedy masterpiece and lamented Chaplin's "misuse" of Brando and Sophia Loren.

In *Reflections in a Golden Eye*, Brando replaced originally-cast Montgomery Clift. It was an unsuccessful attempt by director John Huston at transferring a delicate Carson McCullers story to the screen, noteworthy only because it teamed Brando with Elizabeth Taylor under Huston's direction. It was the first time that Brando had accepted second billing since *A Streetcar Named Desire*.

Brando's best film in years, *The Night of the Following Day* (1968), was overlooked by both critics (except for *Time*) and public. A low-budget, tense and effective melodrama, it co-starred Brando with Richard Boone and Rita Moreno. Many of the scenes seemed to be improvised.

Brando's 1970 film, *Quemada*, garnered more than the usual amount of in-production publicity. As in the past, Brando was in conflict with the director, this time Italian *auteur* director Gillo Pontecorvo *(Battle of Algiers)*. The theme of the film, appropriately, deals with revolution.

Brando in three non-rebel roles.
With Pat Hingle in *The Ugly American*.

Checking a camera set-up on *Bedtime Story*.

The "obligatory" beat-up scene, this time in *The Chase*.

Brando with "good girl" hostage Anjanette Comer in *The Appaloosa*.

(Before its release in the United States its title was changed to *Burn!*) Brando said in an interview in *Life*, referring to the director, "I really would like to kill him."

Although Brando's films in the sixties were disappointing, most film critics defend him by saying that he is the most exciting American actor in films. He gives the impression of rising above the material. He was an *original* and has been so copied by now that the original has been driven to self-parody. Brando's originality is interpreted today as eccentricity.

Since the beginning of his career Brando said it was only a means of earning a living so that he could devote his time to worthy causes. In the sixties, Brando was vociferous concerning civil rights in general and the problems of the American Indian in particular. He has been talking for years about making a film about the American Indian situation. He is a man of honest convictions, who quietly devotes his time, energy and money to causes in which he believes.

In the late sixties Brando refused the starring role in Elia Kazan's *The Arrangement*, announcing that he wanted to devote his time to working on social problems. *The Arrangement* would have reunited him with mentor Kazan. Speculation at the time was that Brando, disappointed with his recent films, was not willing to risk the possible ultimate disappointment of a personally unfulfilling Kazan-Brando film. (Kirk Douglas took over the role, but the film was a critical and commercial disaster.)

Controversy has raged for the last fifteen years over Brando's returning to the stage. Theatre buffs feel that he has "sold out." Theatre critic Harold Clurman said, "We tend to think of him as a 'useless' good actor—that is, one with no real interest in acting for the sake of acting, not acting as a social force."

But film critic Pauline Kael said, "Hollis Alpert lumbered onto the pages of *Cosmopolitan* to attack him [Brando] for not returning to the stage to become a great actor—as if the theatre were the citadel of art. *What* theatre? Was Brando really wrong in feeling that movies are more relevant to our lives than that dead theatre which so many journalists seem to regard as the custodian of integrity and creativity? David Susskind was shocked that a mere actor like Brando should seek to make money, might even dare to consider his own judgment and management preferable to that of millionaire producers. Dwight MacDonald chided Brando for not being content to be a craftsman: 'Mr. Brando has always aspired to something Deeper and More Significant, he has always fancied himself as like an intellectual'—surely," Miss Kael concluded, "a crime he shares with Mr. MacDonald."

Brando's impact as a rebel and as a movie star was

John Saxon, a juvenile romantic lead in the fifties, made a "comeback" as a villain and character actor via *The Appaloosa.*

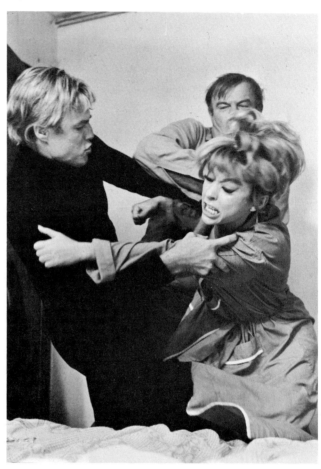

Brando, Jess Hahn, Rita Moreno in *The Night of the Following Day,* a small, underrated film in Brando's late sixties period.

Brando and director Gillo Pontecorvo on the set of *Burn!*

Brando, in costume as Emperor Napoleon for *Desiree*, meets real-life Emperor Haile Selassie of Ethiopia.

so great that no actor of the fifties and sixties could escape comparison.

While James Dean was accused of aping Brando's style, Paul Newman was often compared to Brando in physical appearance. It was a comparison Newman did not appreciate. He once said, "I wonder if anyone ever mistakes him for Paul Newman. I'd like that."

Newman was established as a major movie star after *The Long Hot Summer*. Next he starred in *Cat on a Hot Tin Roof* with Elizabeth Taylor and Burl Ives. "Newman is perhaps the most resourceful and dramatically re-strained of the lot," wrote *New York Times* critic Crow-ther. "He gives an ingratiating picture of a tortured young man. Miss Taylor is next. She is terrific as a pant-ing, impatient wife, wanting the love of her husband as sincerely as she wants an inheritance."

Paul's next was a nebulous comedy, *Rally Round the Flag, Boys*, again with wife Joanne. After the 1959 production *The Young Philadelphians*, for Warners, New-man bought himself out of his film contract for $500,000

and returned to Broadway. (Early in the game, film nov-ice Newman had earned his off-scren rebel stripes by telling off his employer, Jack Warner.)

With Geraldine Page, Newman electrified Broadway in Tennessee Williams' *Sweet Bird of Youth*, which opened March 10, 1959. Walter Kerr, in reviewing Williams' play, described the Chance Wayne character as "an ambigu-ous figure, half vulgar greed, half yearning idealism. . . ." Perhaps if the 1962 film version had been made eight years later, when the language and plot of the play needn't be compromised for film censorship purposes, *Sweet Bird of Youth* might have been a powerful film. However, with plot and language watered down, even though Newman and Page effectively recreated their stage roles, the film was disappointing in all respects. Paul Newman had finally hit his stride in films in 1961 with *The Hustler*.

In *The Hustler*, the character of Eddie Felson, played by Paul Newman, was not the traditional rebel hero. But the powerful story by Robert Rossen and Sidney Carroll, direction by Rossen, and Newman's portrayal, produced a critical and commercial hit film with an amoral, un-savory hero. In *The Hustler*, the girl who leads the hero into soul-searching which eventually provides him some measure of self-respect, was not the stereotype Priscilla Lane-Natalie Wood "good girl." The character of Sarah Packard, portrayed expertly by Piper Laurie, was an alco-holic tramp whom the hero casually meets and becomes physically involved with, before becoming emotionally entangled. Felson is a professional pool player, and when his gangster boss pressures Sarah she commits suicide.

Eddie and Sarah heralded the changing sixties version of the rebel hero and his courageous heroine.

As the *New York Times* critic said, "There may not be much depth to the hero, whom Paul Newman violently plays with a master's control of tart expressions and bitterly passionate attitudes. Nor may there be quite enough clarity in the complicated nature of the girl, whom Piper Laurie wrings into a pathetic and eventu-ally exhausted little rag. But they're both appealing people; he in a truculent, helpless way and she in the manner of a courageous, confused and uncompromis-ing child."

Newman, Miss Laurie and everyone concerned with the production, especially George C. Scott as the evil gangster and Jackie Gleason as Minnesota Fats, was lauded in the reviews. Archer Winsten said *The Hustler* returned Robert Rossen to the company of filmmakers to be reckoned with.

The Hustler was the story of a small-time pool shark (Newman) who makes it to the big time but loses to the champ, Minnesota Fats (Gleason). He then takes up with Miss Laurie, and after having his thumbs broken when

115

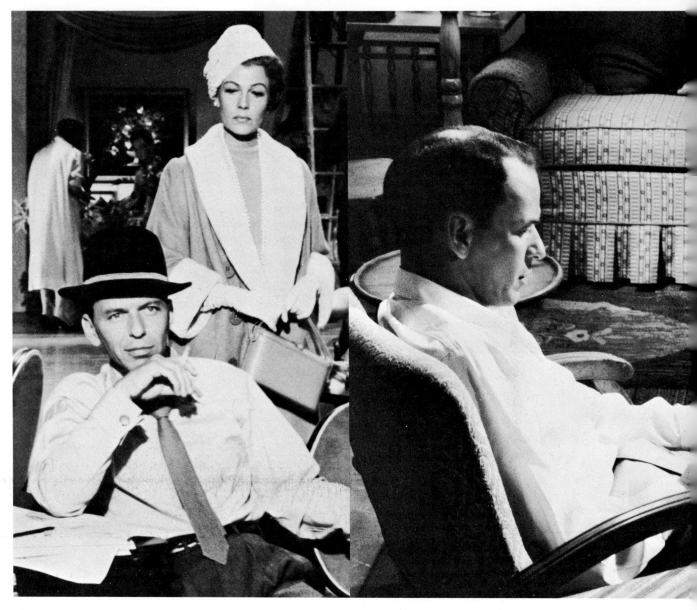

Sinatra in the late fifties and early sixties. Here with Rita Hayworth in *Pal Joey*.

With Shirley MacLaine in *Some Came Running*.

caught hustling in a pool hall, he joins up with gambler-promote Scott. Scott causes Miss Laurie to commit suicide, and Newman realizes he must break with him and stand on his own. He leaves the gamber and wins the return match with Fats. (The ending was reminiscent of Rossen's *Body and Soul.*) "He has lost his love, but he has gained his courage, his character and his integrity," observed Archer Winsten.

The Hustler proved that American film audiences of the sixties were ready to accept an American leading man as a hero with the characteristics of a heel who did not have to die or be reformed at the film's end.

The Hustler paved the way for the rebel anti-heroes of the decade.

With *The Hustler*, Newman proved that he could easily bounce back and forth betwen traditional heroes, rebel heroes, anti-heroes and even villains.

That same year, 1961, marked the screen debut of Warren Beatty. His controversial personality and soul-searching style of acting won instant response from a public hungering for a new, young leading man.

In a career that has spanned less than ten years, and after only a handful of films, Warren Beatty is estab-

116

With Spencer Tracy in *Devil at Four O'Clock*. In *Some Came Running*, Sinatra was an anti-hero, a sensitive writer caught between compassion, logic and reality. Unwilling to compromise, it was certain he would be crushed.

lished as a superstar. Even before his first film, *Splendor in the Grass*, was released, Beatty was a celebrity and off-screen rebel. Although he did not portray a rebel hero in that film, it was one of the most auspicious film debuts since Brando in *The Men*.

Beatty had been discovered by playwright William Inge and starred in Inge's ill-fated Broadway play, *A Loss of Roses*, with Betty Field and Carol Haney. Although the play flopped, Beatty's talents were not overlooked. Walter Kerr said, "Mr. Beatty's performance is mercurial, sensitive, excellent." Kenneth Tynan in *The New Yorker* noted, "Mr. Beatty, sensual around the lips and pensive around the brow, is excellent."

Beatty signed a non-exclusive contract with MGM. In the meantime, Inge had written *Splendor in the Grass*, an original script for director Elia Kazan to star Beatty.

Billing for the film said, "Starring Natalie Wood and introducing Warren Beatty in his very first picture—A Very Special Star." (Warners had used identical billing for James Dean in *East of Eden*.) *Splendor in the Grass* received much in-production publicity because the two stars were reportedly carrying on a highly colorful off-

Paul Newman, with Burl Ives as his father,
in *Cat on a Hot Tin Roof.*

Paul Newman, with Elizabeth Taylor as his wife,
in *Cat on a Hot Tin Roof.*

screen romance, although Natalie Wood was married to Robert Wagner at the time. The press had given much coverage to Beatty's previous romance with Joan Collins, and when Natalie and Wagner separated, Miss Collins switched her attentions to Mr. Wagner.

Splendor in the Grass was a hit, critically and commercially. *Life* said Beatty was "a new and major movie star, combining the little boy lost charms of the late James Dean and the smoldering good looks of Marlon Brando."

As often happens with screen debuts, many people contended that the actor was type-cast and might not be able to play other roles. Archer Winsten, the *New York Post* critic, disagreed, and observed, "A tribute to Kazan's teaching skill is the way in which Warren Beatty handles his lead role in what is his first film and one of his first acting jobs. Ten years of intensive work put in by a notable talent could not improve upon this particular characterization. Even if he has been typecast, the way in which he projects his personality and emotions in front of the camera is an amazing achievement for a young man so lacking in experience."

Beatty's second film, co-starring Vivien Leigh, *The*

Roman Spring of Mrs. Stone, in which he portrayed an Italian gigolo, netted him disastrous reviews.

His third film, *All Fall Down,* presented Beatty in what might be considered his first rebel hero role. The rebel hero of the 1960s had changed. The audience liked the character for his roguishness and daring, would even like to identify with him, but could not feel sympathetic, as they had with Clift in *A Place in the Sun,* Brando in *The Wild One* or Dean in *Rebel Without a Cause.*

All Fall Down was based on James Leo Herlihy's novel, and once again Beatty had talented co-stars (Eva Marie Saint, Angela Lansbury, Karl Malden, Brandon de Wilde), an excellent director (John Frankenheimer), and a sensitive screenplay by William Inge.

Perhaps the plight of American youth searching for a new hero in the sixties can best be exemplified by characters portrayed by Brandon de Wilde. In *All Fall Down* and *Hud,* de Wilde idolizes a new kind of hero, a heel. He questions the validity of this non-heroic hero.

De Wilde had achieved fame as a child, first on the stage and then in the film version of *Member of the Wedding.* In 1953 he had to choose between traditional

Newman, Geraldine Page recreated their stage roles in the disappointing film version of *Sweet Bird of Youth*.

Paul Newman in *The Hustler*. The rebel hero in transition.

hero Van Heflin as his father and anti-hero Alan Ladd as the good-bad guy in *Shane*. Now, portraying the teenage brother of Warren Beatty in *All Fall Down*, de Wilde's choices were not as clearly defined. Angela Lansbury and Karl Malden, as the parents of the two brothers, were presented as a dominating mother and an alcoholic father. Beatty, as Berry-Berry, portrayed a rebellious no-good and de Wilde, as his brother Clinton, was an uncommitted note-taking observer. He saw in Berry-Berry glamour, freedom, independence.

The catalyst in the story is Echo O'Brien (Eva Marie Saint), an older woman who comes into their lives. Clinton has a crush on her, and she intelligently and affectionately develops it into a friendship. He is happy when she falls deeply in love with Berry-Berry, who seemingly returns her love. But Berry-Berry is incapable of loving, reveals himself as the heel he is, and Echo commits suicide. Her death triggers the realization for Clinton that his brother is an unfeeling bastard. What he considered strength is actually a sickness. Berry-Berry "hates life." No longer shackled by a distorted idolatry for his brother, he can now leave Berry-Berry to his own misery.

119

On *The Hustler* set, Paul Newman gets pool lessons from world champion Willie Mosconi.

Paul Newman, Piper Laurie in *The Hustler*. It was a dramatic change of pace for the former glamour girl.

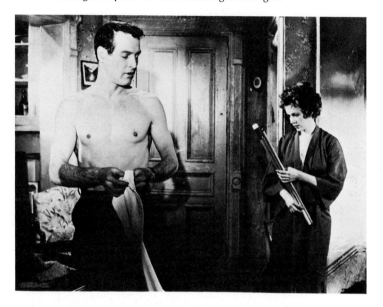

George C. Scott, Piper Laurie, and Paul Newman.

The film was a critical hit but a commercial disaster. Some insight as to why it was a failure was provided by Archer Winsten: "To place this picture accurately inside the mainstream of American film production, it attempts to show people as they are, not as an audience would enjoy having them be. They don't change much, neither for better or worse. And what they are leads inevitably to results which are not the wishful thoughts that please an audience."

Newman, beaten and knuckles broken, is comforted by Piper Laurie.

Beatty received generally good reviews. Stanley Kaufman in *The New Republic* said, "Physically, Beatty has the requisite magnetism. Emotionally, he has the coiled-snake tension of black lower middle-class frustration." Archer Winsten said, "The performances are of a quality too fine for characterization, and they extend right across the board of the top roles. Perhaps the most difficult of the lot is Beatty's careless-on-the-outside, victim-of-himself charm. He does it with the skill and subtlety that marks his rise from role to role to a position of genuine artistic strength."

And Paul V. Beckley in the *New York Herald Tribune* said, "Beatty's performance is the finest of his career."

Bosley Crowther again disliked Beatty, and called him a "Brando or Dean copier." Ironically, Crowther thought *All Fall Down* was terrible but incorrectly predicted its commercial success.

The following year de Wilde again portrayed a youth searching for a heroic hero while being fascinated by a heel. In *Hud,* de Wilde, on the brink of manhood, must choose between the values of his upright grandfather and those of his low-down uncle. *Hud* was, as Judith Crist described it, "about the disintegration of a household through the total amorality of one of its members." This statement also applies to *All Fall Down*. In describing *Hud,* Crist gives us a perfect portrait of the "hero" of the sixties: "Paul Newman's creation, Hud, [is] a hard-living luxuriating carouser, unable to take a woman gently or drive a car slowly. But more important, he is a soulless man, who not only remarks that he doesn't give a damn—but doesn't, involved with neither kith nor kin, devoid of principle, devoid of responsibility, driven only by lust. With our Freudian-inspired insistence on explanation, we speculate on the motivations of this

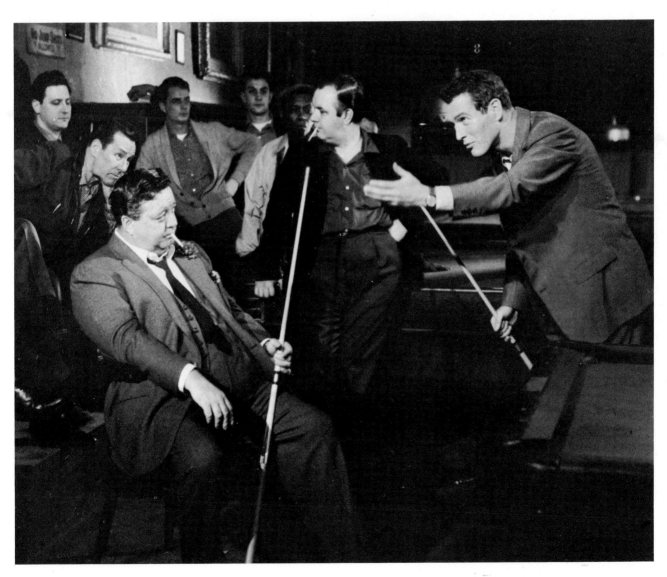

Jackie Gleason (as Minnesota Fats) and Paul Newman.

Warren Beatty, Vivien Leigh in
The Roman Spring of Mrs. Stone.
Beatty's reviews were disastrous.
It was the first—and so far, only
—film by stage director Jose Quintero.

Beatty, Natalie Wood in
Splendor in the Grass.

Pat Hingle, as Beatty's father in *Splendor in the Grass*. Another superlative Kazan supporting cast.

man only to learn that his amorality is not a defense against the world, the exterior of guilt, the hunger for love. The explanation isn't given as Hud shrugs off the last possible human link allowed him and leaves us with a knowledge of depravity and, worse yet, the realization that this man is of our day and of our society.''

The screenplay was by Irving Ravetch and Harriet Frank, Jr., based on a novel by Larry McMurty. Martin Ritt directed and co-produced with Ravetch.

In addition to Newman and de Wilde, the superb cast was headed by Patricia Neal and Melvyn Douglas. Crist continued: "Hud's father, Homer Bannon (Douglas), has long known this enemy, his younger son, and he too has

Zohra Lampert, Warren Beatty in *Splendor in the Grass*. He marries her after his world drastically changes.

Karl Malden, Beatty, Angela Lansbury, Brandon de Wilde and Eva Marie Saint in *All Fall Down*.

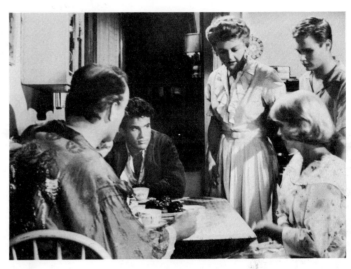

De Wilde, fascinated by brother Beatty's life style in *All Fall Down*.

Beatty, Eva Marie Saint in *All Fall Down*. She was top-billed.

124

Paul Newman, Melvyn Douglas in *Hud*.
The hero as cold-blooded bastard.

no answer. Of Homer Bannon, a cattleman who will not surrender the principles of honesty that have guided his life or an inch of his land or head of cattle to appease his raging offspring, Melvyn Douglas creates a monolithic figure, huge in its stolidity and its integrity but uncomprehending, unyielding. And on the other side of Hud stands Lon, his seventeen-year-old orphaned nephew (de Wilde) brimming with the uncertainties and sensitivities of adolescence. Torn by respect and affection for his grandfather and by the dash and masculinity of his uncle, the boy gropes his way toward personal values.

"The fourth member of the household is Alma, the housekeeper, a careworn but vibrantly mature woman, beautiful created by Patricia Neal. She has the warm heart and cool hand for the boy, the knowing eye and inner response for Hud. "I've done my time with one cold-blooded bastard; I'm not lookin' for another," she warns him, but she is female enough to know the limits of resistance. Miss Neal's portrait of a woman who has lived the hard way and retained compassion, dignity and soul, is superb."

Hud, of course, is not a hero, and not a rebel hero, but in this middle sixties period, with the transition of the rebel hero, the character found wide acceptance. He was aptly described as "a cold blooded bastard."

Newman has said that to him, Hud made the statement that people sometimes grow up at a tragic expense

Patricia Neal, Paul Newman in Hud.
The "good girl" by this time was worldly and worn.

to other people. The actor thought many critics missed the point of Hud's tragic flaw—not giving a damn about anyone else. But in general he was mistaken, since most critics understood the film, the off-beat casting of Newman and his excellent portrayal.

The award-winning ad campaign for the film had a key line, "Why Hud?" which referred to the line where the youngster de Wilde asks, "Why pick on Hud, Grandpa? Nearly everybody around town is like him." *Time* said the producers "created a kind of new-wave Western, using simple realism as their strongest tool."

The climax of the film comes when Homer Bannon's herd contracts hoof and mouth disease, and despite Hud's protestations (he wants to sell the diseased herd to an unsuspecting buyer), the old man has the herd destroyed. Hud's eventual seduction of Alma, with whom the boy is smitten, hastens de Wilde's decision, after his grandfather's death, to leave the ranch, Hud, and Hud's way of life.

Throughout the picture there is a growing awareness of evil on the part of de Wilde. Throughout, Hud is a heel and there is no thought of reformation. Arthur Knight, in the *Saturday Review*, said Ritt "uses Newman's considerable personal magnetism first to cover, then reveal the shallow, egocentric, callous nature of Hud." Knight also said, "*Hud* could stand with *Shane* as an

authentic document of one aspect of the West. In this age of heel-heroes and beasts that walk like men, the screenwriters have pulled a switch that is both commercial and commendable. They have created in *Hud* a charming, raffish monster who demonstrates by inversion that such old-fashioned virtues as honesty, loyalty and filial duty are still highly cherishable."

At the end of the film, the flashiness and swagger of Hud is eclipsed by the righteousness of his father. After the old man's death, and after Alma and finally de Wilde have left him, Hud is alone. "But Hud," Crist concluded, "who shrugs off humanity, stands in triumph alone—as he has stood in their midst. But this is no cynical conclusion that the bastards inherit the earth; it is a shattering recognition of their existence and their ability to flourish among us. This is the triumph of the film, its refusal to sweeten or soften the truth and, above all, its truth-telling in terms of unforgettable people."

And Stanley Kaufmann noted that de Wilde's part was similar to his role in *All Fall Down:* "Adulation that withers and leaves him free."

The creation and audience acceptance of "heel-heroes" and "non-hero heroes" in the late fifties and early sixties, were vital links to the rebel hero tradition in films.

Newman, Brandon de Wilde.

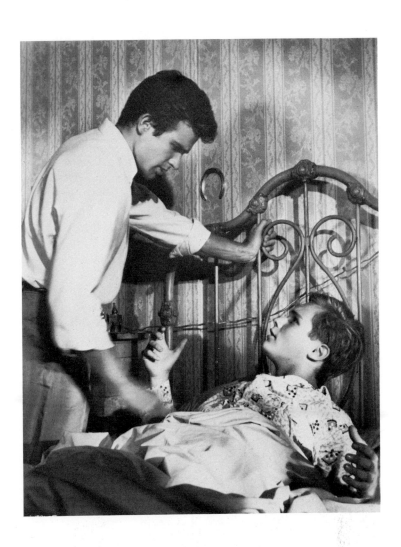

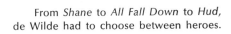
From *Shane* to *All Fall Down* to *Hud*,
de Wilde had to choose between heroes.

7
The Middle Sixties: The Seeming Decline of the Rebel Hero

The youth of the late fifties and early sixties, in their search for new kinds of rebel heroes, discovered Steve McQueen—first on television, later in films. McQueen's distinct personality made him magnetic; youth could relate to him.

Like Garfield, the rugged yet sensitive rebel characters McQueen portrays come remarkably close to reflecting his actual background and off-screen life. To say that many of the roles he has played might have been drawn from his own experience (*The Great Escape, Baby the Rain Must Fall, Nevada Smith*) is an understatement. He spent an unhappy childhood and a wandering, adventurous and reckless youth.

He was born Terence Steven McQueen on March 24, 1930, in Indianapolis. His father deserted the family soon after. He lived with his grandparents in Missouri until he was eleven. Then his mother remarried, sent for him, and with his stepfather they moved to California. Steve became a problem child and his parents sent him to a home for wayward boys (Boys Republic in Chino, California). He made one attempt to escape, failed, and stayed there for almost two years.

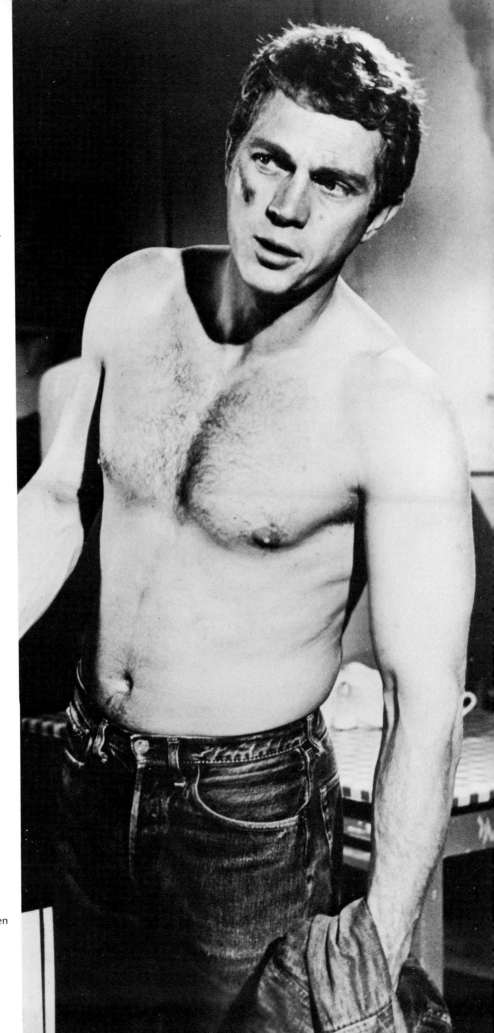

Steve McQueen

In one of his earliest films, *The Blob*,
he was billed as Steven McQueen.

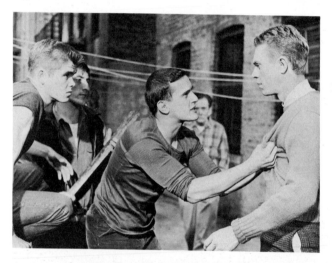

A young Steve McQueen in *Never Love a Stranger*,
with Anthony Franke and Gino Ardito. Robert Stevens directed
the Harold Robbins production, based on Robbins' novel.
An Allied Artists release, the film starred John Barrymore, Jr.

After rejoining his mother, who had by this time moved to New York, he ran away again and joined the crew of a tanker. He abandoned that pursuit in Texas and labored in the oil fields there, worked for a traveling carnival, and ended up in a Canadian lumber camp. He also worked as a runner for a brothel in Port Arthur, Texas—"I had the prettiest chick there."

He enlisted in the Marine Corps in 1947, went AWOL and served forty-one days in the brig but was honorably discharged in 1950.

Landing in New York in 1950 and undergoing an apprenticeship of the typical variety of jobs most young actors take on (salesman, bartender, etc.), he decided to become an actor. He worked in summer stock and early television. In 1956, he was a temporary replacement for Ben Gazzara on Broadway in *A Hatful of Rain*, opposite Vivian Blaine. But his big break came in 1959 when he was cast by Dick Powell as a bounty hunter in the network television show, "Trackdown." Powell recognized McQueen's rare combination of innocence and toughness and saw in him the character of an offbeat underdog. That one episode of "Trackdown" became the pilot show for a new television series, "Wanted: Dead or Alive." The bounty hunter, portrayed by McQueen, was the hero. Bounty hunters are usually "bad guys," but McQueen made the character believable and sympathetic.

The *New York Herald Tribune* said, "The new series is unique insofar as its hero is cast in an unconventional mold. . . . The central character is a bounty hunter, which means that he's an unofficial lawman who follows the reward trail and whose motives are mercenary rather than moral. . . . Steve McQueen, who plays the unsavory hero, follows the pattern of most Western television leading men in that he is a personable young unknown who will try to establish his own identity through the character of Josh Randall."

Steve McQueen became the first rebel hero of the television screen who would make the transition to films.

His first three films, made before his hit television series were *The Blob*, science fiction; *Never Love a Stranger*, teenage gangs; *The Great St. Louis Bank Robbery*. They were not notable.

His first film of note was *Never So Few* (1959), which starred Frank Sinatra, who recognized McQueen's potential. Paul V. Beckley in the *New York Herald Tribune* wrote, "Steve McQueen looks good as a brash, casual GI sergeant who overpowers two military policemen so neatly Sinatra gets him transferred to his outfit. . . . He possesses that combination of smooth-rough charm that suggests star possibilities."

The Magnificent Seven, with Yul Brynner, followed, which presented McQueen as a youthful henchman. After *The Honeymoon Machine*, his first attempt at

Robert Wagner, Steve McQueen in *The War Lover*.
McQueen seemed type-cast in war films early in his career.

McQueen and Sinatra in *Never so Few.*

Sinatra, Steve McQueen in *Never so Few.*
McQueen could have become a member of "The Clan," but didn't.

McQueen, Paula Prentiss, Brigid Bazlen, Jim Hutton
in *The Honeymoon Machine,* an innocuous comedy.

comedy, McQueen returned to a typical rebel role in *Hell Is for Heroes* (1962), as a busted noncommissioned officer staving off a German attack although risking court martial. "An arresting performance by Steve McQueen, a young actor with presence and a keen sense of timing, is the outstanding feature of *Hell Is for Heroes*," said *The New York Times*.

The *Times* continued, "McQueen sharply outlines a provocative modern military type. Surly and unpredictable, a dangerous misfit among the normal soldiers in his platoon, he is the kind of antisocial citizen unable to function in a civilized society.

"But, at the moment of combat when decisive action must be taken, it is his socially adjusted comrades who hesitate, while the maladjusted private takes command. For better or worse, he is the stuff of which heroes are made.

"While the point is never articulated in Mr. McQueen's laconic dialogue, it is entirely clear to the audience. Under Don Siegel's highly skilled direction, it gives strong thematic weight to an unusually well-made film."

After *The War Lover* in 1962, McQueen received fine reviews for his performance in *The Great Escape* (1963). He again received top billing, as he had in *Hell Is For Heroes*. He played an American soldier frequently in solitary confinement in a German prison camp. He was assigned to distract the prison guards by a spectacular motorcycle ride so that the great escape would be successful.

More important than the reviews for *The Great Escape* was the public's reaction to McQueen. The film established him as a movie star and a leading man.

Following *Soldier in the Rain* (1963) with Jackie Gleason and Tuesday Weld, he had the opportunity to star opposite the decade's leading screen ingenue, Natalie Wood.

A poignant tale of a musician and a girl, both Italian-Americans, *Love With the Proper Stranger* was the story of this young couple facing the problem of an illegitimate child and abortion. In the film, McQueen played a sixties kind of rebel. He used in his characterization all the casual yet crusty hip sophistication that Sinatra had introduced to the screen a few years earlier. Most reviewers found fault with the execution of the plot, but McQueen and Natalie Wood were well received. *Newsweek* said, "The performances of both Natalie Wood and Steve McQueen are brilliant" and predicted "it would be only reasonable to expect Academy Award nominations for both of them." Miss Wood in fact received a nomination, McQueen did not. But his career was in full swing. *Newsweek* observed, "McQueen's splendid amalgam of blinks, furrowed brows, smirks, quick smiles, pursed lips, shyness, cat-like grace, and occasional clumsiness is one more explosion of the four-part firecracker of his career for the year."

Steve McQueen and cast, in Don Siegel's *Hell Is for Heroes*.

Steve McQueen, Fess Parker in *Hell Is for Heroes*.

Nick Adams, Steve McQueen in *Hell Is for Heroes*. McQueen portrayed a sarcastic cynic.

Steve McQueen in *The Great Escape*.
The film catapulted him to stardom.

Foote wrote the screenplay, based on his own play, "The Traveling Lady." The play had flopped in 1954. But after Foote adapted the very successful *To Kill a Mockingbird* in 1963, he and that film's producer-director team, Pakula-Mulligan, decided to revive *Baby the Rain Must Fall* and tailor it to the personality of McQueen.

Because of the people involved, it was an eagerly awaited and much-publicized project. But the reviewers were practically unanimous in their dislike of the film. It was a slice-of-life story about a shiftless rock and roll singer (McQueen) married to a decent girl (Remick). Nothing much really happens. There is a great lack of communication between the characters. McQueen was somewhat miscast. As Wanda Hale said in the New York *Daily News*, "McQueen, a fine comedian with a disarming smile, wasn't chicken when he took the part of poor Henry, sadsack, ill-fated, emotionally immature.

"This vital actor just isn't the type to portray such a long-suffering fellow whose life is frustrated, his musical

McQueen in *The Great Escape*.

Natalie Wood was apparently the perfect mate for the screen rebel in the fifties and early sixties, having earlier appeared opposite James Dean in *Rebel Without a Cause* and Warren Beatty in *Splendor in the Grass*.

After *Love With the Proper Stranger*, which cemented his status as a Movie Star, McQueen went into brief, self-imposed retirement and resumed his off-screen rebel career. He had in the past been persuaded to give up professional car racing but he continued to race motorcycles. Drag racing on public highways in New York had almost killed him on several occasions but he continued to race in the Mohabi desert and in Europe with American teams. Newspapers and magazines publicized this to the extent that McQueen's rebel image was firmly entrenched in the minds of the American public.

"Proper Stranger" director Robert Mulligan cast McQueen in his next film, *Baby the Rain Must Fall* (1965). Lee Remick was his leading lady. McQueen by this time had become important enough to form his own company, Solar, Inc., for tax advantages and to gain "some creative control, some artistic leverage."

Solar co-produced the film with Alan Pakula. Horton

talent repressed by a brutal foster mother who has him under her control after he is married and is the father of a five-year-old child.

"Even after her death, he must live by her decree; attend night school to learn a trade and give up singing and guitar playing in local gin mills. Finally rebelling, Henry, a parolee who did time for a stabbing, is sent back to prison."

Lee Remick, and Don Murray as a friend of the family, received fine reviews. But concerning the film, Judith Crist said, "We are left with a dull mixture of unfulfilled suggestion, unrelieved gloom, sordid half-plotting and, above all, pretentiousness, with an Elmer Bernstein score to match and underline the obvious. And *Baby the Rain Must Fall* becomes as banal as the ballad that is its title song."

Archer Winsten's analysis: "The picture's source of dissatisfaction is equally a factor in its air of plot truthfulness. You want something good to happen, or at the

Jackie Gleason, Steve McQueen mug it up on the set of Blake Edwards' *Soldier in the Rain*. The film flopped.

Steve McQueen, Natalie Wood in *Love With the Proper Stranger*. Miss Wood played opposite many rebel heroes.

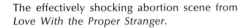
Herschel Bernardi, Steve McQueen in
Love With the Proper Stranger.

The effectively shocking abortion scene from
Love With the Proper Stranger.

very least something conclusive. Instead, the plot dribbles away at the end with everyone departing to separate fates barely suggested. You can hardly guess what's going to happen to each, although you can suspect it won't be good in one case, and shouldn't be too happy in the other. Author Foote has avoided the heavy hand of black tragedy and he has been stern in his rejection of happy solutions.

"Great, but does it have to rain all the time, baby, just because the rain must fall? I mean, this is a truth that leaves you wishing it were a little different, and that's not a good feeling. It doesn't even give that classic catharsis of a whopping personal disaster that allows everyone to cry a bucket and end up all dried out."

In the sixties, newspaper headlines proclaimed McQueen "the King of Cool." They called him the "now" generation Bogart and the first genuine movie star of the decade.

Despite his off-screen rebel image, McQueen's personal life seemed to remain stable for many years. To date he has been married only once, since 1956, to Neile Adams. Miss Adams was a dancer who McQueen met when he was in *Hatful of Rain* and she was in *The*

Natalie Wood, Bernardi, McQueen
in *Love With the Proper Stranger*.

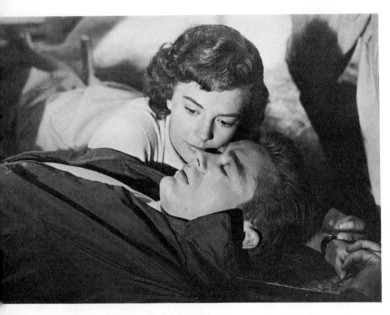

Natalie Wood was "good girl" to many rebel heroes: James Dean—

Warren Beatty—

Pajama Game, on Broadway. After their marriage, she was quoted as saying, "I've never been exposed to that type of man before. I'd been brought up in convents and suddenly this wild man was in my life."

In the summer of 1970, the McQueens announced their separation, but by 1971 they were reconciled. They have two children—a daughter, Terry Leslie, and a son, Chad Steven.

McQueen has returned to car and motorcycle racing, after a studio-enforced layoff. "I enjoy racing in any form," says McQueen, "because the guy next to me couldn't care less what my name is. He just wants to beat me.

"At the start of my racing I had to prove myself. A lot of people think that actors are a little strange, unmasculine, not like the guys who are riveters at Lockheed and things like that. I had to beat the actor's image."

Now, McQueen says, he's past the point where he "must prove anything—my ego or my masculinity. The only reason I race now is because I enjoy it."

McQueen scoffs at writers and amateur psychologists who question him on the supposed connection between racing and the death wish. "Death wish?—I mean, why would I have a death wish?"

Probably because of his unhappy childhood, McQueen seems very family-oriented and has devoted much time and money to helping unfortunate youngsters.

Despite *Baby the Rain Must Fall,* his career did not lag. In 1965 and 1966 he starred in two hit films, *The Cincinnati Kid* and *Nevada Smith.*

In *The Cincinnati Kid,* he portrayed a gambler who overplayed his luck. The characters and story were very similar to *The Hustler,* except that the competitive element was poker instead of pool. Norman Jewison directed from a screenplay by Ring Lardner, Jr., and Terry Southern, based on a novel by Richard Jessup. Although some critics thought the film too slow, most were impressed by the dramatic intensity in the scenes between McQueen as The Challenger and Edward G. Robinson as The Champ.

Tuesday Weld played the sweet young girl who loves McQueen, and Ann-Margret played a married woman who lusts for him. The rest of the impressive cast included Karl Malden, Rip Torn, Joan Blondell, Jack Weston, Cab Calloway, and Jeff Corey. The film was shot in color, and the locale was New Orleans. Although it was considered a "man's movie," it appealed to a large audience, particularly because of McQueen's characterization of the offbeat hero.

In *Nevada Smith,* McQueen recreated the type of role he had played in "Wanted: Dead or Alive." The film had an exciting premise. It was the story of a young half-breed who hunted down his parents murderers. John Michael Hayes' script was based on the Nevada

Steve McQueen

Steve McQueen as the itinerant rock and roll singer in *Baby the Rain Must Fall*.

Steve McQueen, Lee Remick in *Baby the Rain Must Fall*. Many critics thought he was miscast.

Steve McQueen, Ann-Margret, Karl Malden in *The Cincinnati Kid*.

Steve McQueen, Tuesday Weld in *The Cincinnati Kid*.
She's the good girl who lends him money when he's down and out.

Steve McQueen as The Cincinnati Kid, a hustler of poker instead of pool.

Steve McQueen in *Nevada Smith*. Alan Ladd created the role of Nevada Smith in *The Carpetbaggers*.

Steve McQueen, Arthur Kennedy in *Nevada Smith*.

Smith character in Harold Robbins' *The Carpetbaggers*. The film was panned by critics, but was a commercial success. McQueen played more of an anti-hero than rebel hero. *The New York Times'* Vincent Canby said, "McQueen is tightlipped, craggy and believable in the title role. He receives excellent support from the large cast, including Karl Malden, Arthur Kennedy, Martin Landau and Brian Keith."

In all of his films, though many of them received poor reviews, McQueen, like Beatty, has been surrounded by exceptional supporting players.

"I don't have much scope as an actor," he has said. "My flexibility isn't terribly wide. There are certain things I can do, but when I'm bad I stink."

He has shrugged off all comparisons with Bogart or other bygone stars.

"I'm myself," he has said. "I don't see anyone identifying with any of our past greats. They were something to many then; they are something to many now, and I think that's great."

A distinctive personality made McQueen a superstar, but he also possesses the well-honed tools of the actor's trade.

While McQueen's career built steadily, Warren Beatty, after an explosive debut in films, had proved by 1965 to be a critical and box-office disappointment. He did not

141

Steve McQueen, Raf Vallone in *Nevada Smith*.

A young Warren Beatty and Joan Collins at a film premiere.

Warren Beatty, Kim Hunter in *Lilith*.
Beatty and director Robert Rossen had no rapport.

lack job offers, but he was extremely independent and selective. He had turned down leads in *PT 109, By Love Possessed* and *Youngblood Hawke*. In retrospect these were obviously wise decisions, since the films were bad and unsuccessful. He also had been mentioned for the lead in *The Leopard* and *Look Homeward Angel*. And he consistently made news because of his reported high salary demands and his flamboyant off-screen romances.

After a lengthy entanglement with Natalie Wood, he became involved with Leslie Caron. Her husband, Peter Hall, named Beatty correspondent when he divorced Miss Caron.

Though Beatty had turned down films which proved to be failures, his selection of vehicles in the middle sixties also proved to be box-office disappointments. From the beginning, Beatty was a difficult actor to work with. He was always concerned with all aspects of production and, like Brando, had his own ideas on filmmaking.

The first script Beatty decided to do after *All Fall Down* was *Lilith*, under the direction of Robert Rossen. From the start, there was friction, and the final product was a mishmash poorly received by critics and at the box office.

Judith Crist and Joseph Morgenstern were the only two major critics to like Beatty and Arthur Penn's *Mickey One*. The film was shown at the 1965 New York Film Festival and later that year it opened commercially.

Morgenstern in *Newsweek* called *Mickey One* an estimable American film and predicted that it might be even more highly esteemed in countries where English is not spoken.

"It has the 'European' look, the sound and rhythm of profundity. It is stunningly put together and uncommonly well played, especially by Warren Beatty as a nightclub comic whose future is as black and uninviting as outer space."

In the film, Mickey doesn't know how, where or when—he has transgressed the underworld law of the 'mob.' He is pursued by invisible, avenging forces: is it the mob or is it his own nameless guilts arising from his own nameless crimes?

"Who owns me?" he asks early in the film. Morgenstern said the answer was clear: "He will take possession of himself and his fate when he realizes that his guilt cannot be expiated because it does not exist. He needs the courage to shake off his phantoms and confront himself as a mixed human being, not a flawed titan. Mickey, then, is the increasingly familiar existentialist hero, picking his way through the minefields of modern life with no charts to guide him and only a receding North Star burning meaninglessly in the moonless night."

Morgenstern went on to say, "Beatty's performance is original and occasionally brilliant, with little of the self-indulgence that has marred his earlier work."

Peter Fonda, Jean Seberg, Beatty in *Lilith*.

143

Bosley Crowther disagreed: "Mr. Beatty is affected and oddly amateurish in the way he presents the emotional torments and startled reactions of his heel. Shapeless and superficial, his chap generates little sense of real psychological disturbance with which one can have sympathy."

Judith Crist recognized the brilliance of the film: "This very contemporary film, dealing in allegorical terms with the burgeoning terrors of our time, introduces us to some fresh and deeply impressive talents, talents that blend into the co-operative artistry that is movie-making at its best. Plot and dialogue, performance and score communicate in aural and visual terms a story on two levels that throbs with immediacy on both . . . Warren Beatty, so long over-mannered and under-revealed, emerges brilliantly as the Mickey who is 'guilty of not being innocent,' smooth and fast on the routines, suddenly a quivering lump of terror, furtive-eyed, without trust or hope until he finally admits that he hasn't the guts to keep running scared."

Beatty on the run in *Mickey One*, Arthur Penn's film which was an analogy to the McCarthy era.

Beatty as the nightclub entertainer in *Mickey One*.

144

Crist called this Penn's most "creative" film and said he "used Resnais-like techniques in probing memory and experience, in alternating between past and present, repeating the scene, the remark, the mood that has significance. Thus he transcends the literal and in true cinematic style rounds out the story by suggestion, by abandoning chronology, by restoring to total experience.

"*Mickey One* is not a simple film in either the telling or the viewing. It makes demands upon its audience. It is a rich film—belying its under-$1 million budget—and its rewards are equally rich."

The film, produced and directed by Penn, was a box-office disappointment, but technically innovative. It introduced the use of incongruous music over a scene of extreme violence—a plaintive jazz love theme was played while Beatty was being beaten by thugs.

Beatty followed *Mickey One* with two nondescript films in 1966, *Promise Her Anything*, a drab comedy co-starring Leslie Caron, and *Kaleidoscope*. Neither film enhanced Beatty's career or his screen rebel image.

Montgomery Clift, Lee Remick in Elia Kazan's *Wild River*.

Clift, Monroe in *The Misfits*. "He's the only one I know who's worse off than I am," said Marilyn.

Clift, Marilyn Monroe, Clark Gable in *The Misfits*. Production ran way over schedule.

145

Clift, Susannah York in John Huston's *Freud.*

in 1960, but Clift at this juncture was beyond playing leading men. In John Huston's *The Misfits* (1961), written for Marilyn Monroe by Arthur Miller and starring Clark Gable, Marilyn and Clift, Clift portrayed a pathetic, lonely, past-his-prime bronco buster who had fallen on his head once too often. It seemed ghoulish of Miller to write a chilling scene in which Clift is speaking long-distance to his mother and telling her she would not recognize his badly beaten-up face.

Clift was superb in a "cameo" role as a feeble-minded victim of the Nazis in Stanley Kramer's *Judgment at Nuremberg* in 1961. He received an Academy Award nomination as Best Supporting Actor, but the Oscar went to George Chakaris for *West Side Story.*

Clift was fine in the title role of John Huston's *Freud* (1962). But his poor health caused many delays in production, and the final negative cost of the film made it almost impossible for it to realize a profit.

In the remaining four years of his life, Clift made only one picture, *The Defector,* filmed in Munich. It is reported that Elizabeth Taylor was instrumental in launching that film, with the understanding that she would then star opposite Clift in *Reflections in a Golden Eye.* *The Defector* was a low-budget spy story about a United States scientist (Clift) who aids a Russian scientist in defecting to the west. Clift died of a heart attack in New York City before the film's release.

Although only forty-five when he died, Montgomery Clift had become a myth. He projected qualities deeply meaningful to film audiences. But in the end he had been trapped by his need for the public and the demands of the myth. He no longer had the physical appearance, the youth, or the range of acting ability to believably portray the supersensitive, hopelessly doomed hero, a role that is intrinsically youthful.

But Hollywood, being what it is, wouldn't cast him as anything else. Even his next intended vehicle, *Reflections in a Golden Eye,* would have had him as a supersensitive, frustrated man. That Brando would replace him was entirely predictable.

Clift's acting style, although imitated by thousands of tortured young men, was unique. With the exception of Brando, he was possibly the best American film actor of the postwar years. He died too late for the good of his legend. James Dean had died at the right moment, before the youngsters in America became hip, before sexuality on screen was shown and not implied, before he was supplanted by the hipper newcomers—Steve McQueen, Paul Newman, and Warren Beatty. But part of Clift's acting style lives on in each of these men. Unlike Marilyn Monroe, Bogart and Dean, Clift has not attracted garish posthumous adulation. Nevertheless, he affected a generation of film actors, as well as a generation of filmgoers.

That same year, 1966, on July 23, one of the screen's leading rebels, Montgomery Clift, died at the age of forty-five. He had just completed his seventeenth film, *The Defector.* In the eight years since *The Young Lions,* Clift had completed seven films. Although they were all "A" pictures with top directors, Clift never regained the star stature he had enjoyed in the fifties. And in the later films he did not play rebel hero roles. He was an idealistic reporter in *Lonelyhearts* (1959), in which his introverted mannerisms negatively dominated his acting style. Elizabeth Taylor arranged for him to play the lead opposite her in Joseph Mankiewicz's film of Tennessee Williams' *Suddenly, Last Summer,* in which Clift was competent portraying a psychiatrist. But the film belonged to the female stars, Taylor and Katharine Hepburn.

Elia Kazan directed Clift and Lee Remick in *Wild River*

146

Clift, at the beginning of his career—and toward the end.

8
The British Rebel Heroes

In the sixties, while the rebel hero character in Hollywood films was undergoing changes from rebel to anti-hero to non-hero, British films were enjoying a renaissance of critical and commercial success and had introduced the English version of the rebel anti-hero.

With the success of such vehicles as *Room at the Top*, in which the leading man (Laurence Harvey) was a no-good opportunist, and John Osborne's play and subseqeunt movie, *Look Back in Anger*, in which his character Jimmy Porter epitomized the angry young man in post-war Britain caught up in egotism and protest, British films and heroes entered a new age of realism.

In the sixties, social rebellion against the British Establishment was not only evident in drama and films but in fashion, music, language and politics. The rigid social structure in England, and the economic hardships in Britain following World War II, had been smoldering for years and the Establishment was an easy target for rebellion.

The versatile and nonconformist Albert Finney is the most important actor to emerge from Britain in the last decade. After training at the Royal Academy of Dramatic Arts, stage work in London's West End, and a small part in Tony Richardson's film, *The Entertainer*, which starred

Laurence Harvey in *Room at the Top*. An early "hero"-heel.

young actor (Albert Finney), a new sensation of the British stage and screen, is a very exceptional specimen in the run of the working class. Maybe he has an uncommon share of humor, courage, pride and dignity. But he certainly is a satisfying person and a happy, comforting relief from the devious, self-pitying rogues and weaklings we have seen in a lot of modern-day films."

Rachel Roberts and Shirley Anne Field co-starred with Finney in *Saturday Night and Sunday Morning*, directed by Karel Reisz and produced by Tony Richardson. An attitude of social rebellion was combined with intense lustfulness in sordid scenes between Finney and Rachel Roberts. Especially when they were conspiring to make love or trying to arrange an abortion, the camera was used expertly; it crowded them during these taut moments, and revealed pathetically trapped people.

Hollis Alpert called Finney a remarkable actor and said he was "type-cast to perfection on one hand, and presumably unaware of the camera on the other."

The film represented the changing mores in British society. *Films in Review* said, "[the film] has had a greater impact on British audiences than either *Look Back in Anger* or *The Entertainer* . . . (Screenwriter) Alan Sillitoe has said that he is not interested in politics but

Laurence Olivier, Finney next starred in the London stage version of *Billy Liar*. He made it clear that he would not tolerate inattention when one night, faced with a noisy audience, he suddenly stopped performing and said, "I'm up here working, so if you won't shut up, go home, and if you won't shut up or go home, I'm going home." Reportedly, the audience became silent and no one left.

Finney turned down Sam Spiegel's offer to play the title role in *Lawrence of Arabia*, because it involved a long-term contract in Hollywood. The young rebel exploded into international stardom with his first film starring role, *Saturday Night and Sunday Morning*, released in April 1961.

Archer Winsten called it the best British picture of modern times and said, "It had seemed to this observer that England's 'angry young men', judged by past performances, were more petulant and complaining than angry. This picture corrects the lack, presenting in Albert Finney an all-male, high-humor anger the exact likes of which has never before been seen on a screen. The person jumps out at you with the thrill of much recognition in what he is and does. You can hardly understand half of his dialect wordage, but there's never an act or a gesture that doesn't ring the bell of the young laboring buck equally at home in a Nottingham factory or Bridgeport, Conn., or Gary, Indiana."

Bosley Crowther said, "Maybe this sturdy young fellow, who is brilliantly realized and played by a fine

Laurence Harvey, Simone Signoret in *Room at the Top*.
The film brought them both to the attention of American audiences.

An early publicity shot of Richard Burton. Burton had played an angry young man in Osborne's *Look Back in Anger*.

that if he were he would be a Communist. Many of the throw-away lines in *Saturday Night and Sunday Morning* derive from the Communist Party 'line,' as does much of the critical acclaim for this picture, in which Finney is called a 'hero of our times'. It seems to reflect the attitude of that part of contemporary British society which feels the Arthur Seatons (Finney) have a case. Hence the current British indulgence toward delinquency and other forms of a general loosening of discipline. 'Saturday Night' reflects this indulgence. In fact, all of its characters who in any way represent authority—the police, the foreman, the neighborhood gossip—are ridiculed.... It will be interesting to watch the future development of Woodfall Productions ... We shall no doubt soon see whether the 'Saturday Night' of free cinema is to be followed by a 'Sunday Morning' of conformity and the exploitation of a decadent society's preoccupation with sexation."

Another British film rebel emerged in 1965, when muscular Irishman Richard Harris, after completing *Mutiny on the Bounty* with Marlon Brando, and after refusing to be lured into any more "meaningless spectaculars," starred for director Lindsay Anderson in *This Sporting Life*, produced by Karel Reisz.

Reminiscent of Brando characters, Harris portrayed Frank Machin, a Yorkshire miner who achieves local fame and wealth as a rugby football player. He glories in his brute strength and wealth, but is unable, in his violent, inarticulate way, to express love to the one woman he cares for (played by Rachel Roberts).

Judith Crist captured the film with her perceptive review: "Mr. Harris' Frank Machin is not the schemer of *Room at the Top* or the groping drifter of *Saturday Night and Sunday Morning*. His scope is focused: 'You see something you want and you go out and get it. It's as simple as that.' Thus it has been with his literally smashing success on the football field, in his getting all he wants his money to buy, in his gauging his career and sustaining its battering and shattering rewards. But faced with a woman who does not, who ultimately cannot, love him, he faces destruction of the animalism that has sustained him as the unthinking, crashing, smashing force on the football field.

Crist continued, "It is a fascinating duel—for indeed the plot of this movie is secondary, since it is basically a chronicle of a man's self-examination. It devolves into a duel between the demanding man and the strangely distant widow who yields her home, her pride, her body—but never her heart. There is a smile, a happy moment with her children, a brief second of self-revelation—but the man's hunger, expressed always with a fierce and frightening violence, and the woman's almost somnolent introversion, cut each episode short. These

Shirley Ann Field, Albert Finney in *Saturday Night and Sunday Morning.* The good girl wins him over, but he retains his right to rebel.

are closed lives bound by some strange compulsiveness that is instantly recognizable as a groping of the spirit, a reaching toward the heart that even the brute and the somnambulist experience. Theirs is an unmagnificent obsession, degrading and doomed. . . . Mr. Harris, a black-haired giant who is a remarkable young physical blend of Marlon Brando and Trevor Howard, bristles with the ego and impatience of the man aware of his physical superiority. He warms with naivete and childish charm at his success, bellows in befuddlement at the quicker brains and more venal men about him and can but scream with anguish at his final loss. . . . Mr. Harris' portrait of a present-day hairy ape, a man very much of our time, the physical hero struck dumb before the spirit, stands without rival, an unforgettable figure within a powerful and impressive frame."

Off-screen, Harris, more than any other of the British actors, lives the rebel life. A pugnacious character, it is said he has a bad temper, a penchant for getting into fights both verbal and physical. After the success of *This Sporting Life*, like Finney he turned away lucrative offers and produced a financially unrewarding but admirable play, *The Diary of a Madman.* Harris and Lindsay Anderson adapted the one-character play themselves from a Gogol short story.

Finney, too, had returned to the stage, in *Luther*, a success both in London and New York. Finney subsequently made *Tom Jones* (1963), Fielding's sprawling novel, into one of the most successful costume comedies of all time. It was adapted by John Osborne and directed by Tony Richardson.

Finney returned to a sort of establishment rebel type character in the slick Stanley Donen film, *Two for the Road.* In 1968 he directed and starred in *Charlie Bubbles,*

Albert Finney and Rachel Roberts in *Saturday Night and Sunday Morning.* Finney represented the British version of the Brando-Kowalski-working man kind of rebel.

151

Richard Harris, Rachel Roberts in *This Sporting Life*. The sensitive brute is unable to express the genuine love he feels for the lonely woman.

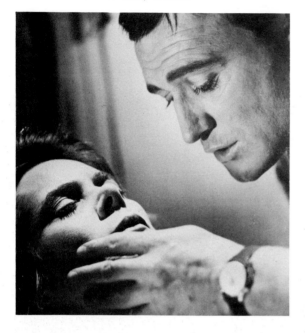

Richard Harris as the soccer player in *This Sporting Life*.

Richard Harris, Rachel Roberts.

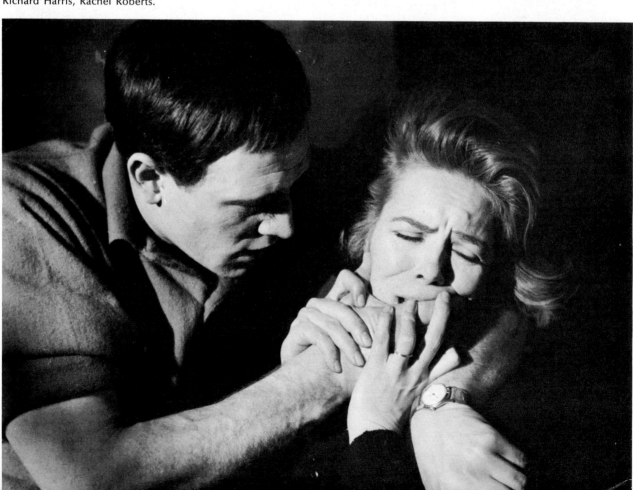

Richard Harris, Rachel Roberts.

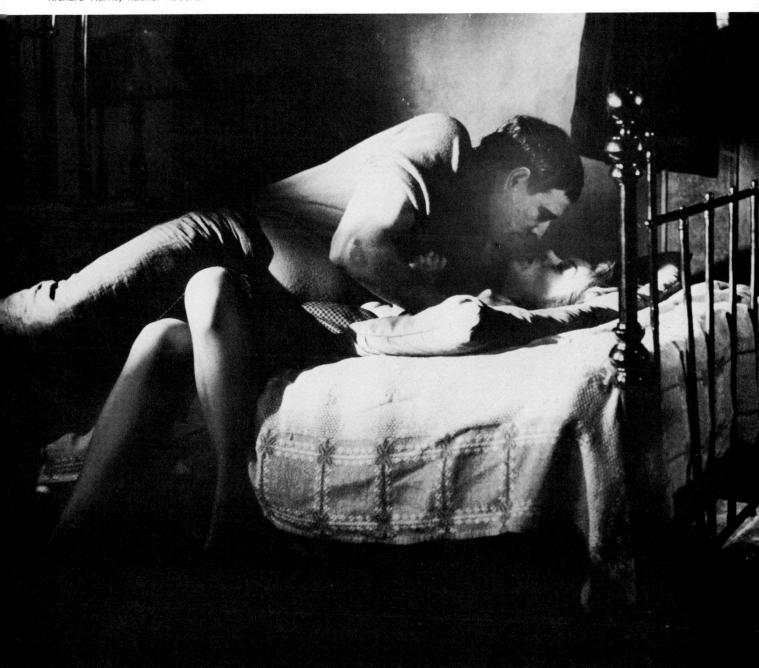

Doris Day, Richard Harris in *Caprice*. One of Harris'
"commercial" American films. It flopped.

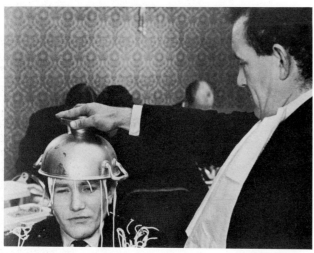

Finney, Colin Blakely in a realistic drunk scene
from *Charlie Bubbles*.

Albert Finney, Audrey Hepburn in *Two for the Road*.
Finney proved, like Brando and Clift, that he could bring
his rebel quality to non-rebel or quasi-rebel roles.

Albert Finney as Tom Jones. The unconventional hero
of the novel was successfully transferred to the screen
by director Tony Richardson.

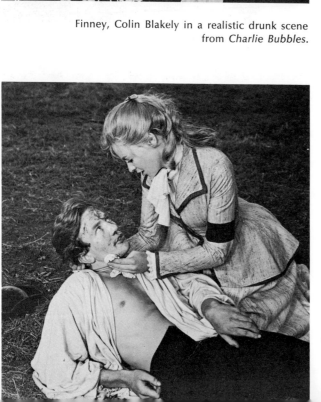

Albert Finney, Susannah York in *Tom Jones*.

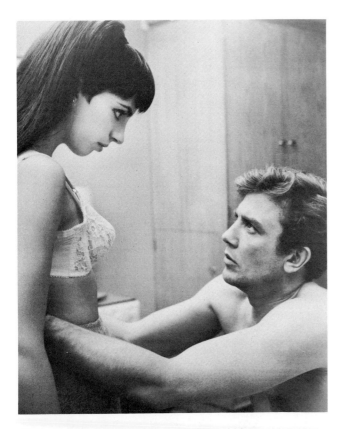

Albert Finney, Liza Minnelli in *Charlie Bubbles*.

Finney directing a scene for *Charlie Bubbles*, described as "a becalmed *Blow-Up*." The film received excellent reviews.

Michael Caine.

produced by Michael Medwin. Finney portrayed a non-hero writer caught up in the meaninglessness of his existence.

He and Medwin were also responsible for producing the low-budget film, *If*, directed by Lindsay Anderson. *If* is a quasi-futuristic account of the cruelties and eventual rebellion in a boys' school, symbolic of the ills and deterioration of British society.

Michael Caine is the third important figure in this list of British rebel/anti-heroes of the sixties. Though his initial success came with *The Ipcress File* (1965), his big hit came the following year, in the memorable *Alfie*. In the former, directed by Sidney Furie, producer Harry Saltzman, who was co-producer of the James Bond films and the Jean-Paul Belmondo detective films, created with Caine a new super-sleuth with human (rather than super-human) qualities, coupled with a be-spectacled midwestern professor look. *The Ipcress File* made Caine a star, and the following year *Alfie* was released. Lewis Gilbert produced and directed Bill Naughton's story of the ultimate heel-hero.

"Alfie," wrote Archer Winsten, "the man of independence who depends on nobody and nobody depends on him, is a monument to self-satisfied selfishness who, once seen and heard, cannot be forgotten. . . . Alfie has one bird in love with him right after the other. They'll

do anything for him. And he will let them. And there's very little he will do for them, except perhaps get them pregnant and be perfectly honest about his intentions. No he has no notion of getting married to anyone.

"When he gets in trouble—a bit of a spot on his lungs—his character is further revealed as less than admirable. But when he gets a married woman in trouble, that's when he can sink down to rock bottom and perhaps to an even lower depth.

"All of this, presented in the best of humor, with complete frankness, with no suggestion that there might be something wrong with him, makes a portrait that is funny, horrible and devastating."

New York *Daily News* critic Wanda Hale gave the film

A scene from *If . . .*, produced by Albert Finney and Michael Medwin, directed by Lindsay Anderson. It was Anderson's second film, following years after *This Sporting Life*.

Michael Caine and Nigel Green in *The Ipcress File*, which established Caine as a star.

Michael Caine, Sue Lloyd off-set during *The Ipcress File*.

Michael Caine, Vivian Merchant in *Alfie*.

four stars and explained, "Vivien Merchant is Lily, whom Alfie meets at the sanatorium, where her husband is taking a long rest cure. Lonely, healthy Lily is easy prey for Alfie. The result, an abortion, hits the audience a stunning blow, even if it is heard from behind curtains and not seen. But it has a moralizing effect on both Lily and Alfie.

"Alfie, quite broken-up by this experience, goes walking alone at night along the docks, ruminating aloud to the audience. 'I've got everything I want but peace of mind. And if you ain't got peace of mind, you ain't got nothing.'"

As the brute egoist, Alfie's only match in the film is Ruby, portrayed by Shelley Winters, a brassy, wealthy woman who uses people just like Alfie does—and eventually drops Alfie for someone younger. Hollis Alpert explains Caine's appeal and why the character wasn't an out-and-out bastard: "Caine understands his character and pervades its enactment with a kind of ironic sympathy. This is particularly important in the case of Alfie, who might have appeared to be somewhat loathesome otherwise. Caine makes Alfie believable and likeable, less a cynic than a man reacting to a perplexing dilemma."

Michael Caine as Alfie. The British version of heel as "hero."

Alfie makes a play for rich American lady, played by Shelley Winters.

Alan Bates as a non-conventional British hero, in *Georgy Girl*.

Terence Stamp in *Blue*. Critics thought he had an ability to project without speaking.

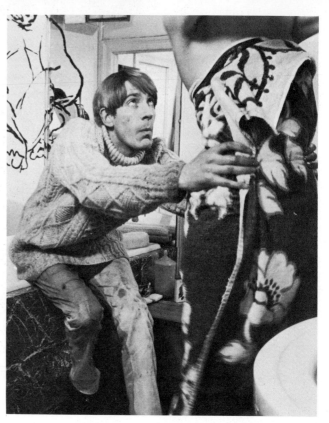

David Warner in *Morgan*. Karel Reisz directed.

The other British actors in the sixties who played rebel roles include David Hemmings in *Blow-Up*, although the film is unquestionably director Antonioni's picture, and Alan Bates, who had impact in *Georgy Girl*.

As the hip, now, with-it mod photographer, Hemmings epitomized the late sixties idea of artistic and social freedom—the ultimate swinger. Bosley Crowther identified him as "completely fascinating—languid, self-indulgent, cool, yet expressive of so much frustration." And Judith Crist said, "Hemmings has made the photographer a world-weary, physically exhausted, cynical but oddly vulnerable young man."

Alan Bates played an irresponsible but irresistibly uninhibited young man in *Georgy Girl*. Like the David Warner character in *Morgan*, Bates represented to the youth of the mid-sixties a screw-it-all, just enjoy life to the fullest and make no commitments attitude.

These British hit films, these stars and the "heroes" they portrayed in the sixties, influenced international moviemaking, while British trends in fashion and popular music revolutionized those fields.

David Hemmings as the mod photographer in *Blow-Up*. He was described as "a combination of the tiger and the baby-faced lone wolf." The mod hero has no concern or understanding for the society in which he lives, hence his difficulty discerning reality from fantasy.

Vanessa Redgrave, David Hemmings in Antonioni's first English language film, *Blow-Up*. Critics said Antonioni handled the new sexual freedom with "delicacy and taste."

9
Renaissance for the Rebel Hero: A New Blend

The rebel character in Hollywood after the death of James Dean went through a period of transition and did not acquire distinct new characteristics until the late 1960s. In the early sixties, President Kennedy and his family had replaced film stars as the country's "royalty" and momentarily replaced them on the covers of most movie fan magazines. For once, the First Family provided the glamour and social life people yearned for. Probably for the first time in a century, the country's youth was involved in politics with such Kennedy projects as the Peace Corps.

After President Kennedy's assassination, the subsequent increased civil rights unrest, and deepening in-

volvement in Vietnam, the youth of the sixties, more vocal than their counterparts in the fifties, became angered over establishment policies and politics. Reactions to suburban affluence and society's objections to legalizing marijuana and other drugs produced a new group of angry young men and women who did more than just talk. The mumbling beatniks of the late fifties were replaced by the articulate, protesting hippies of the late sixties.

The three established rebel/anti-heroes in films in the late sixties were Paul Newman, Warren Beatty, and Steve McQueen.

In 1967, screen audiences were exposed to two new

Paul Newman in *Cool Hand Luke*

Warren Beatty in *Bonnie and Clyde*

rebel hero characters: Luke Jackson, in *Cool Hand Luke*, was a return to a Garfield-like rebel hero, a loner born to lose, a traditionally defiant victim of society but a man full of pride and dignity.

Clyde Barrow in *Bonnie and Clyde* was a villain raised to folk-hero status. An out-and-out murderer and thief, the character in the film was admired just as the real-life Clyde had been admired during the Depression by apathetic and rootless people who identified with a nobody yearning to be a somebody, a rebel without cause—but a man with enough guts to actively strike out against the establishment, even though he did it illegally, unethically, and immorally.

Warren Beatty produced and starred in *Bonnie and Clyde*, one of the most controversial—and successful—films of the decade. Established and respected film reviewers across the country, including Bosley Crowther of *The New York Times*, Joseph Morgenstern of *Newsweek*, and the reviewer for *Time*, misunderstood the film and lambasted it. Even its distributor, Warner Bros.-Seven Arts, did not realize the artistic potential of the film and booked it for quick playoff dates across the country.

But the youth of the country responded to the film, and magazine and *auteur* film critics recognized *Bonnie and Clyde* as an artistic triumph. *Bonnie and Clyde* was a huge hit in Europe. In America, the film evoked emotional response from almost all quarters. Basically, it angered traditionalists, if not consciously than subconsciously, because it presented murdering villains sympathetically. When at the film's end the bodies of Bonnie and Clyde are riddled with bullets for what seems like a ten-minute scene, the viewer is left with a revulsion for the police and a distaste for organized authority.

No one who saw *Bonnie and Clyde* was indifferent to it. Perhaps this is the greatest compliment that can be paid to any work of art. People either hated it and attacked it or loved it and defended it. Hollis Alpert in the *Saturday Review* said, "The film is unusual, and even fascinating, in its depiction of the reactions to the crime wave by people who have no reason to love banks, and of the sheer seeming normality of the way of life of the criminals."

Arthur Penn, who had collaborated with Beatty producing and directing *Mickey One*, directed *Bonnie and Clyde* from a screenplay by David Newman and Robert Benton.

Perhaps the reason *Bonnie and Clyde* appealed to youth was best expressed by *Vogue*. "It is in retrospect that the pathos of this pair, so much a product of their time and so potentially to be parallel in ours, is evident—and this evidence provides the particular distinction of what might well have been just another gangster movie, another glorification of violence and rebellion, another bit of lip-service to morality. Instead, Beatty and Penn and their associates have given us a portrait of a pair of displaced young people on the run, catapulted from one atrocity to another by their neurotic sensualities, terrifying in their complete dissociation from humanity, their aspiration to nothing beyond the satisfaction of the moment's whim."

Bosley Crowther of *The New York Times* completely misunderstood the film. Many people in the motion picture industry think that his review and subsequent re-review, defending his original review, were used by his enemies at the *Times* to oust him. This, of course, was not the first film Mr. Crowther misunderstood. But *Bonnie and Clyde* was a monumental success—it was a trend-setting film whose influence carried over into fashion, attitudes about future filmmaking and film viewing, and even philosophy. To his enemies, Crowther had not only misunderstood the film, he had not perceived a trend.

Within a year, Crowther had left the *Times* and was replaced by *auteur* critic Renata Adler (who herself only lasted a year). Crowther, who had never appreciated Beatty's acting, did not appreciate his producing venture, either. About *Bonnie and Clyde*, he said: "This blending of farce with brutal killings is as pointless as it is lacking in taste, since it makes no valid commentary upon the already travestied truth. And it leaves an astonished critic wondering just what purpose Mr. Penn and Mr. Beatty think they serve with this strangely antique, sentimental claptrap."

The film, before opening in New York in August, 1967, had opened the Montreal International Film Festival. Kathleen Carroll, of the New York *Daily News*, liked the film and correctly predicted, "Viewers will very likely split into two camps. The dissenters will find Arthur Penn's treatment of Bonnie Parker and Clyde Barrow, the outlaw pair who terrorized the Southwest in the thirties, too giddy. They will penalize the director for the way he ricochets from near-slapstick to tragedy.

"It is true that Penn makes the law look like the Keystone Cops or the heavies in a Western. Bonnie and Clyde, at moments, might be cut-ups who skipped out of Sunday school to go on a spree—a bank-robbing spree, that is. And Penn does give the Depression a pseudo-hillbilly beat.

"But the non-dissenters can refute these statements. Penn, without depriving his film of spirit, hasn't missed the gaunt, hungry faces and the desolate towns.

"As his business is illusion not reality, Penn can also be forgiven for making the story of Bonnie and Clyde a folk ballad, and not a gay ballad at that. After bullets first wound the pair, the director deliberately holds up the frenetic action, and suddenly instead of nice kids on a lark, there are two pathetic delinquents, like Frankie and Johnnie, the pawns of fate."

Archer Winsten at the *New York Post*, usually a trend perceiver, was in this case, like Crowther, concerned with the film being fictional and not sticking to the facts about the real Bonnie and Clyde.

Morgenstern devoted less than a column in *Newsweek* to his original review. The following week, however, he had the courage to re-review the picture and say, "Last week this magazine said that *Bonnie and Clyde*, a tale of two young bank robbers in the 1930s, turns into a 'squalid shoot-'em-up for the moron trade' because it does not know what to make of its own violence. I am sorry to say I consider that review grossly unfair and regrettably inaccurate. I am sorrier to say I wrote it."

This time, Morgenstern devoted almost three full columns to his re-review and a discussion of violence. "Seeing the film a second time," he said, "and surrounded by an audience no more or less moronic than I, but enjoying itself almost to the point of rapture, I realized that *Bonnie and Clyde* knows perfectly well what to make of its violence, and makes a cogent statement with it—that violence is not necessarily perpetrated by shambling cavemen or quivering psychopaths but may also be the casual, easy expression of only slightly aberrated citizens, of jes' folks."

And he concluded, "There is, in the depiction of violence, a thin red line between the precisely appropriate and the imprecisely offensive. Sometimes a few too many frames of film may mean the difference between a shot that makes its point concisely and one that lingers slobberingly. These few frames or scenes in *Bonnie and Clyde* will hardly change the course of human events. When we talk about movies, even artistic movies, we are not talking about urban renewal programs, nuclear nonproliferation treaties or rat control bills. Art cannot dictate to life and movies cannot transform life, unless we want to retool the entire industry for the production of propaganda. But art can certainly reflect life, clarify and improve life; and since most of humanity teeters on the edge of violence every day, there is no earthly reason why art should not turn violence to its own good ends, showing us what we do and why. The clear danger, of course, is that violence begets violence in life and engenders confusion in art. It is a potent weapon, but it tends to aim the marksman."

Bonnie and Clyde received ten Academy Award nominations, including Best Picture, Best Actor and Best Actress. After it was initially released and did adequate business, Warren Beatty the producer did what Warren Beatty the actor had always refused to do—publicity. After *Newsweek* and *Time* reconsidered and apologized for their first reviews, Beatty pressured Warner Bros. to

1967 was the year of Beatty and Dunaway as Bonnie and Clyde.

re-release the picture. The film went back into first-run houses, and business was as much as three and four times higher than the first time around.

Although previous films had villains with sympathetic overtones, *Bonnie and Clyde* was the first film success with cold-blooded murderers as the hero and heroine. The film was innovative in technique as well as script. With *Bonnie and Clyde*, film editor Dede Allen established herself as one of the most creative editors of the decade. *Bonnie and Clyde* was the most important influence on male fashions since *The Wild One*'s popularizing of black leather jackets. This can also be at-

Beatty, Dunaway. Director Arthur Penn has said that Bonnie and Clyde attacked the absurdity of their time. They were relevant to 1967 audiences.

Gene Hackman, Beatty,
Dunaway in *Bonnie and Clyde*.

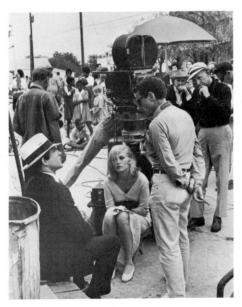

Director Arthur Penn talks with stars Warren Beatty
and Faye Dunaway, shooting *Bonnie and Clyde*.

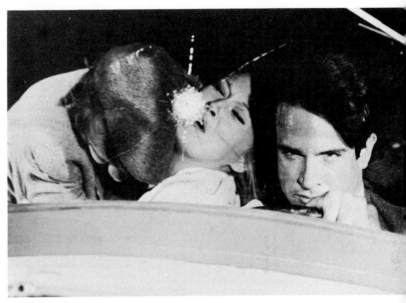

Michael J. Pollard, Faye Dunaway, Warren Beatty.
Bonnie and Clyde's luck begins running out.

tributed to European designers, who picked up on
"Bonnie and Clyde" fashions and led the new fashion
revolt in America. Hats and caps came back into style,
along with wide-lapeled, striped and colored suits and
wide ties.

As they had done in *Mickey One*, Penn and Beatty
used incongruous music over scenes of extreme violence. This time they used happy Blue Grass music.
(Charles Strouse wrote the score.)

With *Bonnie and Clyde*, Penn succeeded in creating an
American folk legend in cinematic ballad form. Clyde
Barrow was a hero that youngsters did not idolize or

want to emulate, but then again no rebel hero ever is.
The rebel hero engenders sympathy and empathy. Youth
identified with Bonnie and Clyde because of their plight
—two small people caught up in "the system."

Luke Jackson as portrayed by Paul Newman in *Cool
Hand Luke* (released in November 1967) appealed to a
wider cross-section of Americans, people of all ages and
from all walks of life, including the critics, because he
was an easier-to-understand rebel. For thirty years America had been exposed to this kind of loner.

Cool Hand Luke received almost unanimously rave reviews. After *Hud*, Newman had appeared in such films as

165

Some of Newman's non-rebel hero roles:
The Prize (with Micheline Presle)—

Hitchcock's *Torn Curtain* (with Julie Andrews)—

A New Kind of Love, The Prize, Lady L and *Torn Curtain.* He had also played a villain in *The Outrage,* a re-make of *Rashomon* set in the old West. (Newman considers it his best performance.) He starred in Martin Ritt's *Hombre* and successfully played an anti-hero, Bogart-like detective in *Harper.*

Cool Hand Luke resumed Newman's career as a rebel. Discussing his type-casting in rebel roles in the sixties, he said, "Few actors can avoid that." He admits he hasn't found as much originality in parts as he'd like— "Depth and detail, yes, but not too much originality." But, unlike Garfield, for the most part Newman is in a position to select decidedly superior scripts.

"Luke is the perfect existential hero," said Stuart Rosenberg, who directed the film. Newman said, "He's the guy who beats the system. Luke is the ultimate non-conformist and rebel. He may be in jail or in the Army or wherever, but he's still a free agent."

Bosley Crowther, who had missed the "hero" aspects in the character of Clyde Barrow, was attuned to the conventional rebel hero of Luke Jackson: "That traditional object of sorrow and compassion in American folk song and lore, the chain gang prisoner, is given as strong a presentation as ever he has had on the screen in *Cool Hand Luke.*

"Indeed, in my recollection, he has never been as forcefully revealed as a victim not only of the brutality and sadistic discipline of his captors, but also—and this is most important—of the indirect cruelty that comes from idolization in the eyes of his fellow prisoners and, finally, of himself.

Crowther continued: "This reticent young fellow who is picked up by the police at the beginning of this film and sent off to a correctional work camp, in what is evidently some Southern state, for the minor offense of vandalizing parking meters, is more than a conventional misused convict, more than a human being who is unjustly accused. He is a psychologically disturbed and complicated victim of his own self-ostracism and pride.

"He is a curiously calculating loner, a terse and sarcastic misanthrope who treats his jailors with taciturn defiance and his fellow prisoners with cool contempt— at the start. He takes with bland endurance the kicks and proddings and verbal insults the guards rain on him, and he smiles when his fellows ridicule him and haze him unmercifully.

"But he has pride and the dignity of detachment grown out of some boyhood hurt, perhaps. He isn't a coward or weakling. So when things finally come to the point that we must fight the top-dog prisoner to a showdown, he does so gamely, ferociously and defiantly until he drops."

Judith Crist said about "Luke," "He is the natural born martyr, the man in revolt for whom the revolution is all."

The Outrage (with Claire Bloom), *Rashomon* in the old West.

Paul Newman as the anti-hero detective, Harper. It was reminiscent of the Bogart films.

Guards Strother Martin and Robert Donner try to physically and spiritually break Luke.
When he cracks, his mates despise him for shattering their heroic myth.

Paul Newman as Cool Hand Luke.

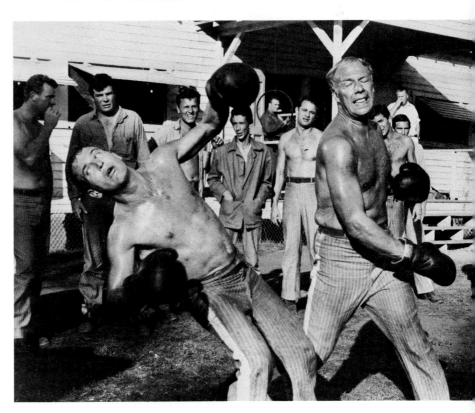

Newman, George Kennedy in *Cool Hand Luke*.

Director Paul Newman with wife and *Rachel, Rachel* star Joanne Woodward.

Newman in *Winning*. A traditional but contemporary hero.

The excellent supporting cast was headed by George Kennedy (who won the Best Supporting Actor Academy Award), J. D. Cannon, Lou Antonio, and Jo Van Fleet.

Newman received tremendous personal reviews and was nominated for an Academy Award. (Both Newman and Beatty lost that year to Rod Steiger in *In the Heat of the Night*.)

Joseph Morgenstern in *Newsweek:* "He is a loner, a refugee from respectability, a drifter: 'I never planned anything in my life.' Yet there is something about him (aside from the fact that he is Paul Newman) which sets him apart. He has a knowing smile and a calm, cool spirit that will not be broken by threats or torture. He has no weapons. Indeed, he becomes a leader only by showing how much punishment he can take from the biggest bully in the prison barracks.

"By extension, he is the existential hero who decides to assert his existence by the very act of deciding. Luke's first decision is to survive. His second decision, which makes him a hero to the other men, is to survive as a man with a private self, not as a docile serf who mumbles cringing homage to his master each time he makes a move.

"Newman catches the man's ironic humor handsomely, and the film has many other details that lift it far above any run-of-the-mine adventure."

Paul Newman, Robert Redford in
Butch Cassidy and the Sundance Kid.

Newman, Redford, Katharine Ross off the set of
Butch Cassidy and the Sundance Kid.

And Morgenstern noted, "The star succumbs to that standard scene (see *On the Waterfront, From Here to Eternity, Mickey One* or *The Chase*) in which the battered hero ends up in a crucifixion pose."

The only departure in *Cool Hand Luke* from the traditional rebel hero movie was the lack of a good girl leading lady, and as Archer Winsten noted, "It is a picture without love, and very short of pretty sentimentality or a happy ending. Nevertheless, it keeps you in there, and when it's over you've seen a man with all the guts in the world, more than's good for him. It makes a picture that is exciting and unforgettable."

Newman followed *Cool Hand Luke* with *The Secret War of Harry Frigg* and *Winning.*

Before *Winning*, Newman had turned to directing with *Rachel, Rachel*, in which he directed his wife, Joanne Woodward. The film was brilliant and Woodward received an Academy Award nomination for her performance. The film was also nominated as Best Picture, but, incredibly, Newman was not nominated as Best Director. (He did win the New York Film Critics' Best Director award, however.)

In *Butch Cassidy and the Sundance Kid*, Newman and Robart Redford, who will perhaps become one of the rebel hero stars of the seventies, starred as unconventional villain/heroes.

Seemingly, of all the rebel hero stars discussed in this book, Paul Newman leads the most conventional life. He is a successful businessman in the film industry, and his rebellion is confined to shunning Hollywood, living with his family in Connecticut and becoming actively involved in national politics. He campaigned strenuously for Eugene McCarthy in the '68 presidential primaries.

Although he had been married once before and has three children by that marriage (Scott, Susan and Stephanie), he has been married to Miss Woodward since 1958. They have three daughters: Eleanor, Melissa and Clea.

Most publicity concerning his offscreen rebellious attitude and offbeat personality centers around his driving a Volkswagen with a souped-up Porsche engine. In his career, Newman has always been a totally disciplined and professional performer.

Warren Beatty, who began as a rebellious star in Hollywood, by now had become much more cooperative, since he had become his own producer. Beatty, still unmarried, continues to shun publicity and leads a *private* private life. With the changing mores of the late sixties, Beatty's life style and love affairs were no longer shocking, therefore no longer headlines.

The decade's third leading rebel hero star, Steve McQueen, after *Nevada Smith*, starred in *The Sand Pebbles*. In that film he played a sensitive American sailor in the Orient during the twenties, groping for meaning in a rather aimless society.

McQueen turned suave in *The Thomas Crown Affair*,

opposite Faye Dunaway (it was her first release after *Bonnie and Clyde*). McQueen used elements of his sophisticated Crown character and combined them with his tough guy characteristics for his role as the hip cop in *Bullitt*. Renata Adler in *The New York Times* said, "McQueen . . . embodies his special kind of aware, existential cool—less taut and hardshell than Bogart, less lost and adrift than Mastroianni, a little of both."

It was a colossal hit, providing audiences with the kind of combination hero they had been prepared for during the last thirty years, a man with rebel/anti-and-traditional hero traits.

In his personal life, McQueen continues to remain an individualist. He manages his career well. "It's a good racket," he says, "And let's face it, you can't beat the bread." He brushes off the suggestion that he may be the hip hero kids are looking for. "I really don't think hero-worship of movie stars is coming back. The movie audience of today is much too sophisticated to adopt any heroes. They might have favorites, but certainly not heroes."

Perhaps today's youth "relates," then, to Steve McQueen, Paul Newman and Warren Beatty.

Steve McQueen in *The Sand Pebbles.*
Though not a rebel role, the film provided McQueen with
the opportunity of proving his box-office drawing power.

McQueen, Candice Bergen in *The Sand Pebbles.*

However, it is more likely that they relate most directly to stars like Dustin Hoffman and Peter Fonda. The most obvious reason is that *they* are, to the youth of the seventies, representative of average looks, average sexual prowess and average ability. Hoffman and Fonda starred in two of the last decade's most contemporary, important, and successful films: *The Graduate* and *Easy Rider.*

With *The Graduate,* what the motion picture industry terms the 18-26 youth market was discovered. In the almost thirty years since *Four Daughters,* the rebel hero of the screen had made the fantastic transition from rebelling against poverty to rebelling against wealth. Of course, in reality he was still rebelling against "the system" and his inability to live within it.

Mike Nichols' film, produced by Laurence Turman with a screenplay by Calder Willingham and Buck Henry, was based on the novel by Charles Webb.

The novel, only semi-successful before the film, concerned a young boy returning to his upper middle-class Los Angeles family from an Eastern university and floundering about while deciding what course his life should take.

The film followed the novel closely except that Nichols had the inspiration to cast an "average" (some thought ugly) looking actor, Dustin Hoffman, as the lead, instead of a blond-haired blue-eyed WASP.

The Graduate was one of the first films about youth shot from a youthful viewpoint instead of from an adult perspective (for example, *Take Her, She's Mine* and *Generation.*)

McQueen as Bullitt, the rebel cop.

Bullitt found a wide audience throughout the world.

The boy, Benjamin, during the summer after his graduation, becomes sexually involved with Mrs. Robinson (Anne Bancroft), the wife of his father's business associate. But he meets and falls in love with her daughter (Katharine Ross) and after many complications woos her away from a pending marriage to someone else. They jauntily jump on a bus and escape her hysterical parents, the groom, and the wedding party.

Hollis Alpert in the *Saturday Review* said, "The freshest, funniest and most touching film of the year . . . about the love pangs of a twenty-one-year-old, filled with delightful surprises, cheekiness, sex, satire, irreverence toward some of the most sacred of American cows, and, in addition, [it] gives us the distinct feeling that the American film may never be quite the same again. . . . As the young man, Dustin Hoffman is the most delightful film hero of our generation. Slightly undersized, totally unsmiling, he stares his way through a series of horrendous, harrowing experiences which lead him from first sex to first real and true love."

Newsweek said, "The film provides an unforgettable portrait of a boy caught in the full panic of self-discovery and dragged screaming into manhood.

"Like many another new college graduate, Benjamin Braddock is alienated. His only distinction is how much he has to be alienated from: a string of scholarly achievements, rich parents, a Beverly Hills home done in California ghastly with materials that God never dreamed of during that heavy week's work, a scuba diving suit, and all of it blighted by a suspicion that his only mission in life is to mope."

Folk-rock stars Simon and Garfunkel wrote the score for the film, and their song "Mrs. Robinson," although not written especially for the film, became a standard.

The film and all the actors received rave reviews, but director Mike Nichols was especially lauded.

The character of young Benjamin Braddock, as portrayed by Hoffman, immediately caught the imagination of millions of alienated young people across the country. The plot and the characters clearly focused on the exact points that many young people of the sixties rebelled against, namely hypocrisy among their elders and discontent with materialism. Benjamin represented urban youth, intellectual, liberal and basically pessimistic. The character was concerned with goals, or lack of them, and communicating.

As always, the rebel hero, unable to work within the current system was searching for values. Again, it is his love for the young "good girl" (Katharine Ross) which leads him on the right path to self-discovery. The twist of having the "evil woman" and "good woman" mother and daughter merely added to the contemporary style of the film.

McQueen, Faye Dunaway in Norman Jewison's *The Thomas Crown Affair*. It was a non-rebel role.

Hoffman was the first Hollywood star since Warren Beatty to become an "overnight sensation." His salary for *The Graduate* was only $20,000. For his next film, *Midnight Cowboy,* he received ten times that amount. By 1970, after *John and Mary,* only his third major film, he was a super-star who could command top salaries and percentages. (While *The Graduate* was running in New York, Hoffman was collecting $55 weekly unemployment insurance.)

Unlike Beatty, with Hoffman there was no major publicity campaign prior to his first film. But after *The Graduate,* Hoffman appeared on the covers of almost all major magazines. After completing *Midnight Cowboy* but before its release, he appeared on Broadway in *Jimmy Shine.* The play was a vehicle for Hoffman, received lukewarm notices (*he* received excellent reviews), and closed when he left the run. He had appeared off-Broadway before this, in *Eh,* for which he won the Vernon Rice and *Theatre World* awards, and *The Journey of the Fifth Horse,* for which he won an Obie.

During the off-Broadway years, Hoffman made one low-budget film in Europe, *Madigan's Millions.* He portrayed a misfit treasury agent. The film was not released in America until after *Midnight Cowboy.*

Hoffman is the only child of Harry and Lillian Hoffman. He was named after silent screen star Dustin Farnum by his stage-struck mother. His father is a successful designer of furniture.

Although he had a series of odd jobs before *The Graduate,* "Dustila," as he is called by his mother, never had to starve.

After *The Graduate* and *Midnight Cowboy,* Hoffman married his longtime companion, non-professional Anne Byrne, who has a daughter, Karina, by a previous marriage.

Like many other rebel hero stars, Hoffman has undergone psychoanalysis. He is an off-screen rebel in the sense that he wants to keep his private life very private. He has said, "What I'm trying to do is keep myself on the ground." Discussing public adulation, he says, "I think that's very dangerous, like what happened to James Dean. Once you become the myth, turn into a public thing, you must get to feel omnipotent—that you can never die."

Many writers of the late sixties found it fascinating to compare the rebel hero qualities of Hoffman with the traditional hero qualities of people like Spencer Tracy, James Stewart and John Wayne. Hoffman's heroes represent alienated, complex people who are losers, where the traditional heroes are always winners, decisive with an unerring sense of right and wrong.

Hoffman may have been speaking for the youth of America and why they reacted to *The Graduate* when he said, "I don't know if psychiatrists agree, but I feel sure

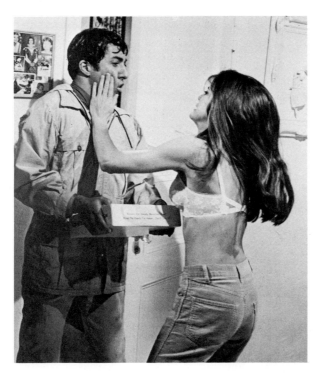

Dustin Hoffman, Katharine Ross in *The Graduate*.

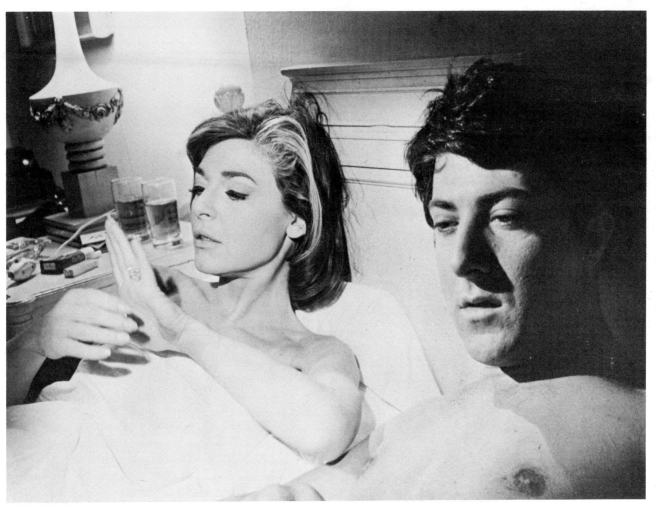

Anne Bancroft, Dustin Hoffman chat in bed in *The Graduate*.

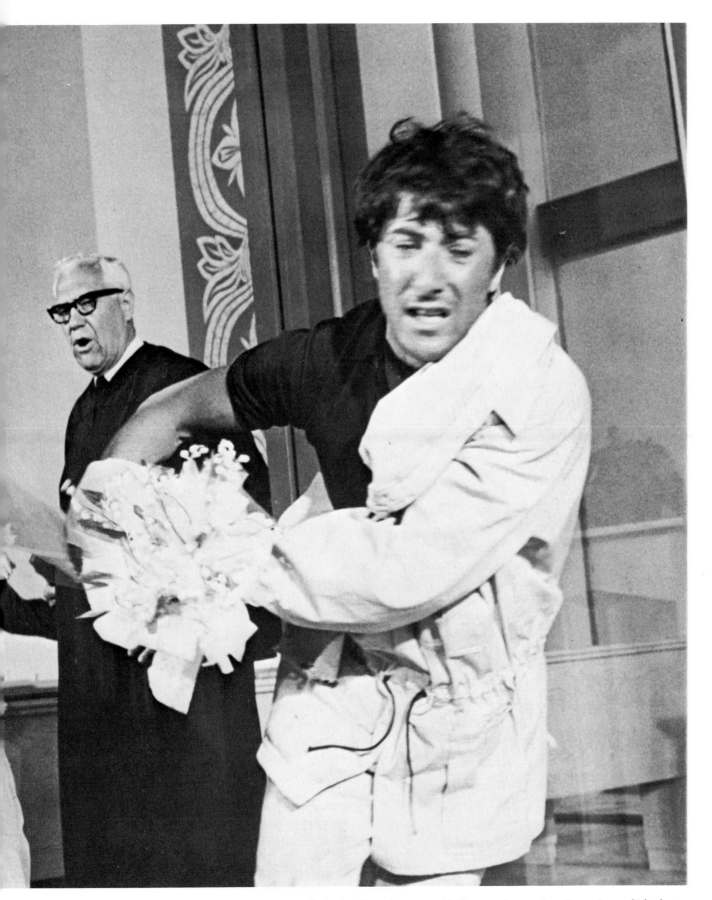

Katharine Ross denounces Hoffman, as her mother (Anne Bancroft) looks on.

that film, more than any other single thing, has damaged America. My parents and their generation escaped the Depression by sitting in movie theatres and allowing themselves to be hypnotized by those images on that great big screen. Many of those movies were about furs and Cadillacs and swimming pools. So it was no wonder they believed that, if they ever broke out of the bread lines, that's where the good life was. Now it's the kids who are forming the backlash. They've had the advantages of all that affluence and they are reacting against it."

In Hoffman's fifth film, *Little Big Man,* directed by Arthur Penn he plays Jack Crabb, an Indian fighter who survives a series of perils and dies at age 111.

Hoffman likes stardom. "I now have the freedom to pick my shots. Stardom equals freedom. It's the only equation that matters." Like the new generation of rebel stars, Hoffman likes the freedom and money but does not enjoy living like a star—and doesn't.

As with most successful films, *The Graduate* inspired imitators. Some were successful (Paramount's *Goodbye, Columbus*), others failed.

The generation gap, the term coined in the sixties to describe the lack of communication between people in

Dustin Hoffman, Mia Farrow in *John and Mary,* the actor's first attempt at a traditional, contemporary young leading man.

different age groups, had narrowed by 1969 so that there seemed even to be a gap between eighteen and twenty-one-year-olds! It was this new, younger, pot-smoking generation that turned on to *Easy Rider.* American-International, the company which had pioneered "youth" films with their innocuous horror and beach bikini movies of the late fifties and early sixties, can be credited with the first socially significant youth films paving the way for *Easy Rider.* In the mid-sixties, American-International, with great intuition and an ear for what was happening in pop music, sensed the spirit of rebellion among America's youth. Protest and protest songs were popular, and American-International jumped on the bandwagon and produced some "protest pictures."

In the mid-sixties, black-leather-jacketed motorcycle clubs were still symbolic of the most rebellious groups. American-International decided on a film about them, *The Wild Angels,* "borrowing" the title from *The Wild One* and the motorcycle group, Hells Angels.

"This ugly piece of trash," as *Newsweek* described *The Wild Angels,* "where aspiring fascists wear iron crosses and decorate their haunts with swastikas, revels in the shock value of murder, mob violence, gratuitous brutality and a squalid rape in a chapel during a funeral."

Significantly, *Wild Angels,* directed by Roger Corman, opened the 27th Venice International Film Festival in 1966—to unanimous critical blasts.

The film opened with a foreword that said: "The picture you are about to see will shock and perhaps anger you. Although the events and characters are fictitious, the story is a reflection of our times."

The film, which starred Peter Fonda and Nancy Sinatra, was disliked by the Europeans because it showed what they considered "too much brutality." It was banned in Denmark. Andrew Sarris in the *Village Voice* noted, "*The Wild Angels* has caused somewhat of a stir on the international scene by being chosen to open the recently concluded Venice Film Festival. We don't have Claire Boothe Luce on hand to instruct Italians in the American Image as she did more than a decade ago when *Blackboard Jungle* threatened to besmirch the glories of our big city secondary schools. *The Wild Angels* is undoubtedly stronger stuff than *Blackboard Jungle,* but the principle is the same. Let's not hang out our dirty linen in public, at least not where the European Left can draw its own diabolical conclusions. There is some virtue if not much validity to this argument. The European Left is now so completely bankrupt intellectually," Sarris concluded "that American self-criticism serves no constructive purpose. In fact, Europeans seem to have picked up every American vice except self-hatred."

In America, the film was a hit with the public, al-

Hoffman created a fascinating character in Ratso, an agile pickpocket conman, in *Midnight Cowboy*.

though the critics panned it. Hollis Alpert said, "Presumably having seen *Scorpio Rising*, Kenneth Anger's experimental film about leather-jacketed motorcyclists, Mr. Corman was moved to make a feature-length study of the creepy breed, employing in his film some of the original models, and also those offspring of screen nobility, Peter Fonda and Nancy Sinatra. Bereft of social purpose, satire, or meaning, *The Wild Angels* strings together such incidents as the invasion of a hospital and the rape of a Negro nurse, a gang fight, and an orgy in a church. American-International, the firm that commissioned this heady screen display, is now busily selling the cozy little film to the impressionable teen-agers of America and the world. Proudly, too."

The Wild Angels was a classic exploitation bike movie and inspired other bike movies (*Hell's Angels on Wheels, Hell's Angels 69, Violent Angels, The Cycle Savages*) which formed a kind of underground folk literature for a certain segment of American youth. The films fabricated a myth to express what this group resented (order and the Establishment) and what they yearned for (excitement, perhaps death). The outlaw leader of the gang was always revealed as an existential hero.

American-International followed *The Wild Angels* with another vehicle starring Peter Fonda, this time opposite Susan Strasberg, *The Trip*, dealing with the drug scene in America, notably LSD. Actor Jack Nicholson wrote the script.

Again, Corman produced and directed, and again American-International broke ground with the first com-

Jon Voight may be one of the rebel hero stars of the seventies.

Jon Voight in *Midnight Cowboy*, with Paul Newman poster on the wall.

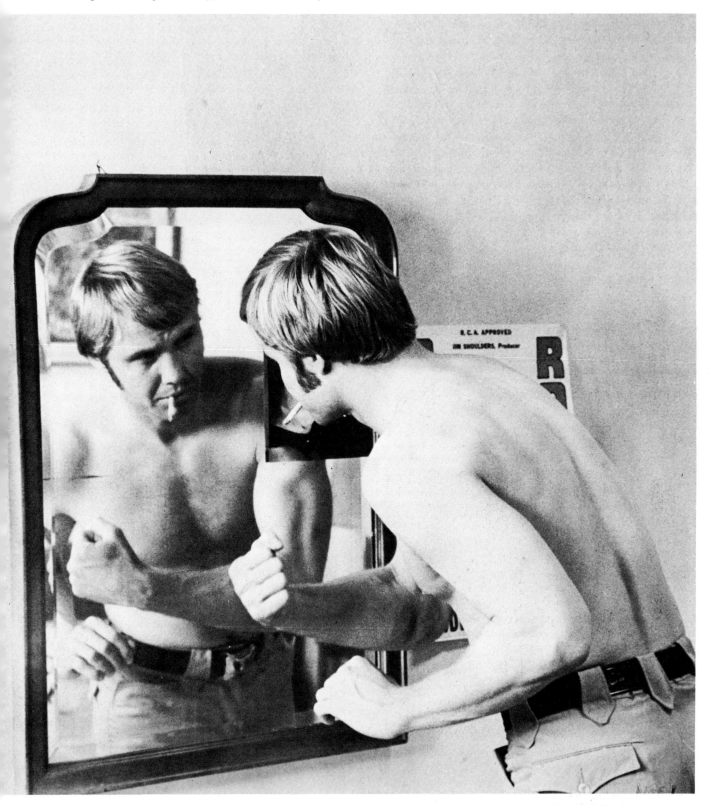

mercial film attempting to re-create an LSD experience. The picture neither downgrades the experience severely to warn audiences against LSD nor praises it highly to tempt them. Archer Winsten said, "There's quite a build-up of scenery and some indication of danger. You're left with some curiosity and some fear and a feeling that this picture by no means exhausts the subject. There must be a lot more to it, both pro and con. Obviously it's not something to be taken lightly, and it's doubtful that this popular version of LSD-taking can be considered medical gospel."

Joseph Morgenstern in *Newsweek* said, "Here is the hippie as hero, with Peter Fonda doing everything a hippie hero should: rejecting all the ... hypocrisy and TV commercials of Western civilization; embracing his peer group's cardinal act of faith, which is that beauty, truth and ultimate serenity lie within each and every one of us, awaiting only liberation at the altar of acid.

"And sure enough, the stuff works. Down and down he goes, round and round he goes, getting to know himself better by the second. The pity is that the hero is as much of a dullard stoned as sober, a nudnik Narcissus with so few spiritual resources that his dreams are just the stuff most movie life is made on."

In *The Trip*, Fonda played a television commercial director who took LSD for greater self-revelations. Fonda said, "Adults hate the flim, but teenagers go for it. 'Trip' is a first-person film, involving the audience, and teenagers want to participate. Adults prefer third-person films.

"Young people fifteen to twenty get an emotional experience with 'The Trip.' Then they're glad it's over.

"Why should a film point out morality?" asked Fonda. "Kids don't like to be lied to while they're being preached at. The generation gap is less now than it was in my father's day. There's no respect if there's no communication. . . .

"They don't believe in the duplicity of mom and dad or authority for authority's sake. Living a lie is the worst kind of symbolism going."

After the film was released, Fonda expressed displeasure because American-International had changed the film's point of view. He said, "It [the final version of the movie] isn't *The Trip* I agreed to shoot. The movie wasn't supposed to be a comment on the use of LSD, but the releasing company got nervous about the reaction of the theatre owners and they added a frozen frame of my face at the end that cracks into a million pieces." He also disagreed with another "compromise," as he put it—the insertion of a prologue. "There's no reason to apologize just because you make a picture on a controversial subject."

Fonda didn't think the film presented a valid portrayal of an LSD trip. "It never gets intellectual, and in that sense it doesn't accurately portray the effect of acid." He said that it isn't the drug but a former environment that causes "a bad trip." "What I mean is LSD turns on the light in a dark room but what shows up in the room was already there. That's what people don't understand. A quest for honesty in society is what the youth rebellion is all about."

Even though the son of Henry Fonda (and his second wife Frances Brokaw) had been in films for years (*Tammy and the Doctor, Lilith, The Victors*) the public hadn't reacted to him as a traditional leading man and he himself was disdainful of these films, their "conventional plots" and "antiquated morality." He also had a reputation as an off-screen rebel, and argued constantly with Warren Beatty during production of *Lilith*.

The American public has the marvelous ability to view an actor in a film and bring to his performance not only the qualities of the character he is playing but all of the actor's publicized off-screen qualities as well. Movie stars (not character actors but stars) as American films have produced them for the last sixty years, project basically their own personalities. Therefore Peter Fonda was unsuccessful as the clean-cut boy-next-door leading man. He needed films like *The Wild Angels* and *The Trip*, and the concurrent revelation of his true character—nonconformist personified, not the Jack Armstrong All-American Son of the All-American Star—to project film characters that youth of America could relate to.

The Trip received poor reviews but was successful and, along with the success of *The Wild Angels*, Fonda finally skyrocketed to stardom.

Fonda was born in New York City on February 23, 1939. He is two years younger than his sister Jane. He is six feet two inches tall, an inch taller than his father. There is a strong family resemblance. Much has been, and will be, written about the Fondas. In recent years, much has been revealed about Peter's and Jane's unorthodox childhoods and Peter's attempt at suicide after he learned of his mother's suicide and while his father honeymooned with his third wife.

Peter attended private schools as a youth. His adolescent years were troubled. He began drinking at fourteen and at sixteen was expelled from an exclusive prep school for punching a teacher in the mouth.

He entered acting via summer stock and the Broadway stage via the play *Blood, Sweat and Stanley Poole*. When he first went to Hollywood, he received the usual publicity buildup and tested for films such as *PT 109*. In the middle sixties, the Fonda children's relationship with their father was revealed to be less than ideal. Jane and Peter began telling interviewers that there was no communication between them and their famous parent.

Unsavory headlines involving Peter appeared in 1965 when Peter's best friend, Eugene "Stormy" McDonald,

23-year-old heir to a $30 million Zenith radio fortune, died violently under mysterious circumstances in Tuscon, Arizona. Fonda and other friends of McDonald underwent lie detector tests in connection with McDonald's suicide.

In 1966, Peter was arrested for possessing marijuana, and his father, ignoring the supposed rift between them, rushed to his side to offer moral support. A *Variety* headline in 1966 read: "At 27, Peter Fonda Parades His Bit: Non-Conformity!"

Even in 1970, Fonda still discussed the fact that he smokes marijuana every day and gives out statements that he and his father disagree on many issues but that finally they are "communicating."

Most of the publicity concerning *The Trip* centered around Fonda's actually having experimented with LSD. He gave out such quotes as: "LSD was a catalyst. It brought me away from one point of view and gave me a million points of view. So I can never accept one point of view anymore. I can never go back home.

"I don't worry about the kids going too far out," he says. "I·respect the youth and the studentship of the campus leaders who are agitating for the sake of agitation, even though that's really just masturbating. I know that they'll come back eventually—through television, through radio; they'll go full circle and get involved just

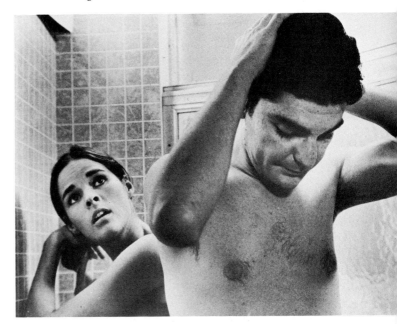

Ali MacGraw, Richard Benjamin in *Goodbye Columbus*, a success riding on the coat tails of *The Graduate*.

through the desire not to get involved. But you can't blame the kids for getting a little paranoidal. Every time they find themselves a hero, someone comes along and shoots him.

"Jack Kennedy had the promise of international qualities. And that's what we have to look for. It's too late for us to be just national. All flags have to go, including the flag on the 18th hole of the country club. As soon as someone has a flag, other people get behind him. Pretty soon they say: 'Our flag's better than your flag. We'll show 'em .Circle the wagons. Follow 'Duke' Wayne. Up the Alamo."

Peter Fonda represents all the new rebel hero stars in that he wants to make sure his "fans" realize he's as rebellious off-screen as on.

The only part of Peter Fonda's life thus far that is non-rebellious and non-controversial is his marriage. He has been married since 1961 to Susan Brewer, who is not an actress. She is the stepdaughter of Noah Dietrich, who was once Howard Hughes' top business aide. The Fondas have two children, a daughter, Bridget Jane, and a son, Justin.

The most important thing to Fonda is producing and directing his own films. Reportedly, he received $50,000 for every million dollars his American-International films grossed. After *The Trip*, Fonda collaborated with longtime friend, actor Dennis Hopper, and with writer Terry Southern, on *Easy Rider*. American-International wanted Corman to direct but the Fonda-Hopper-Sothern team

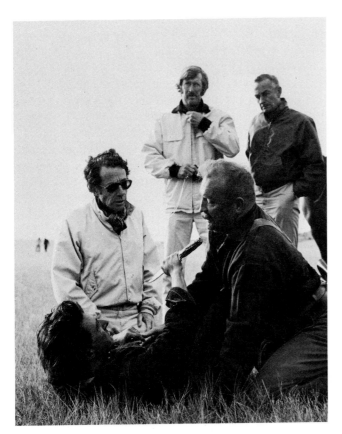

Arthur Penn directing Dustin Hoffman in *Little Big Man*.

The Wild Angels.

Peter Fonda as Heavenly Blues, Nancy Sinatra as Mike in *The Wild Angels*.

Peter Fonda, Susan Strasberg in *The Trip*.

Dennis Hopper, Peter Fonda in *The Trip*.

wanted Dennis to direct. Hopper had directed the desert sequences in *The Trip*.

With almost a compulsion to insist on his individuality, Fonda produced the film himself on a small budget, with Hopper directing. After the film was completed a deal was arranged with Columbia Pictures, who bought *Easy Rider* for $375,000. It has so far grossed over $20 million and made Fonda a multimillionaire, as *Bonnie and Clyde* made Warren Beatty one.

Easy Rider was seen by millions of people of all generations. Fonda likes to compare it with *Rebel Without a Cause* in that youngsters saw the movie, went home, discussed it with their parents and directly or indirectly influenced their parents into seeing the film.

The story for *Easy Rider* originated with Fonda. It concerns two characters, Wyatt (Fonda), sometimes called Captain America, and Billy (Hopper), two dope peddlers who, after making a big sale, cycle from California to the New Orleans Mardi Gras and on to Florida. In their symbolic search for freedom, the two engage in a series of social encounters. There are breathtaking shots of the open country of the southwest and there is an excellent rock score provided by groups such as The Band, The Byrds, Jimmy Hendrix Experience and Steppenwolf.

About half-way through the film they meet George Hanson (Jack Nicholson), an alcoholic Southern misfit. He, however, unlike the two leads, tries to articulate his desire to communicate. He is killed by redneck Southerners who attack the trio, and eventually Wyatt and Billy are slain too. But before that, Wyatt, with his line, "We blew it," expresses the realization that they are not free. They have sold out for money, they have failed. They have betrayed their possibilities. It symbolizes that all leadership in America, including the moral, anti-establishment and supposedly free and honest leadership, has failed too.

The film won a prize at the 1969 Cannes Film Festival as "Best Film by a New Director."

"The amazing, confusing thing about *Easy Rider*," wrote Joseph Morgenstern, "is that it really is eloquent in almost every passage that isn't marked Hush—Eloquence at Work. It's an important movie that's sure to involve a large audience in its story of two . . . decent hippies set upon by indecent squares. . . . *Easy Rider* is a linear descendant of the cheap, violent and topical melodramas that Fonda did for American-International Pictures. . . . *Easy Rider* has the immediacy of these earlier movies, but it uses violence sparingly, to devastating effect. And it develops its single, strong idea through flashes of brilliant writing and performance . . . through dazzling photography (by Lazslo Kovacs) . . . reminds us of how ravishingly beautiful parts of the nation remain."

Laszlo Kovacs was cinematographer and Donn Cam-

Peter Fonda, Sandra Dee in Ross Hunter's film, *Tammy and the Doctor.* It was before Fonda changed his image and achieved acceptance from screen audiences.

Buddies Dennis Hopper, Peter Fonda off-screen during filming of *Easy Rider.*

A scene at the commune in *Easy Rider*.

bern editor after Hopper had "disagreements" with Barry Feinstein, originally set to film *Easy Rider*.

Archer Winsten said, "Seldom does one see a picture that can combine in such just proportions the physical beauty of this world, its conflicts of old violent prejudice with new modes of living and dressing, and the grass culture that bulks so large among the young advanced. If anyone can increase our understanding of this world, it's these makers of the graphic picture. And yet, it's by no means a simplification or popularization. They seem pretty much to have 'told it like it is' and let their thing speak for itself."

Easy Rider became the most talked-about movie of the year. Pot-smoking and drug-taking, which had been explored and exploited in other movies, reached its widest audience with the success of *Easy Rider*. 1969 was also a year in which the legalizing of pot became a

national issue. Jacob Brackman in *Esquire* said, "*Easy Rider* can be dug as phenomenology of turning on. It portrays dope as an integral part, if not quite the focus, of people's lives. Most of its characters' waking time is spent in commission of a felony. Hopper never bothers to 'defend' it—he won't even make invidious distinctions between 'users' and 'pushers.' He and Fonda are scarcely postwar babies. They were born during the Depression and by their age alone seem to stand not for something young and modish and New, but for a persistent, almost tireless approach to organizing one's life.

"It strikes one early on that the actors in the film and, one easily imagines, all the men behind the camera, are truly sucking on Mother Nature's own sweet herb. Material that would ordinarily appear inadvertent seems 'right' in a film of, by, and for the stoned."

Pauline Kael in *The New Yorker* discussed the fact

Peter Fonda, Dennis Hopper, Jack Nicholson in *Easy Rider*.

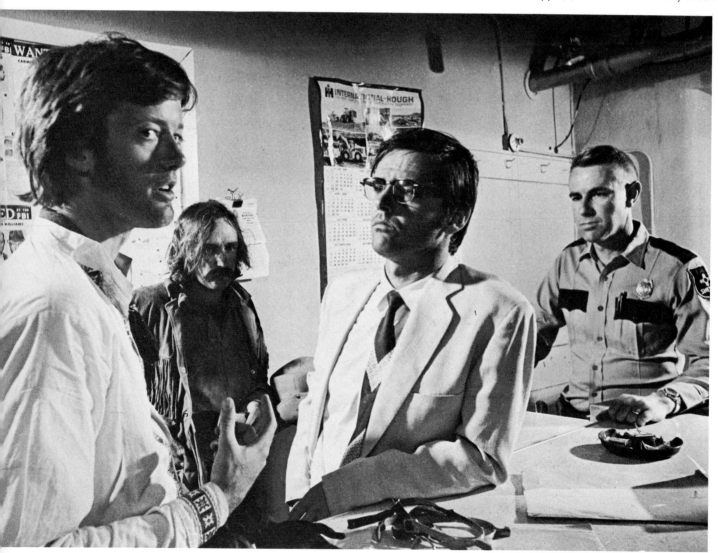

that art houses in America for the first time were being dominated by American movies, and that "the young audiences waiting outside, sitting on the sidewalk or standing in line, are no longer waiting just for entertainment. The waiting together may itself be part of the feeling of the community, and they go inside almost for sacramental purposes. For all the talk (and fear) of ritual participation in the 'new' theatre, it is really taking place on a national scale in the movie houses, at certain American films that might be called cult films, though they have probably become cult films because they are the most interesting films around. What is new about *Easy Rider*," Miss Kael remarked, "is not necessarily that one finds its attitudes appealing but that the movie conveys the mood of the drug culture with such skill and in such full belief that these simplicities are the truth that one can understand why these attitudes are appealing to others. *Easy Rider* is an expression and a confirmation of how this audience feels: the movie attracts a new kind of 'inside' audience, whose members enjoy tuning in together to a whole complex of shared signals and attitudes. And although one may be uneasy over the satisfaction the audience seems to receive from responding to the general masochism and to the murder of Captain America, the movie obviously rings true to the audience's vision. It's cool to feel that you can't win, that it's all rigged and hopeless. It's even cool to believe in purity and sacrifice. Those of us who reject the heroic

central character and the statements of *Easy Rider* may still be caught by something edgy and ominous in it—the acceptance of the constant danger of sudden violence. We're not sure how much of this paranoia isn't paranoia."

The rebel "hero" character Fonda portrayed in *Easy Rider* seemingly had come a long way from the rebel hero of the thirties. Garfield, when he did speak, spit out words of disgust and distaste. The *Easy Rider* heroes mumble about "getting your thing together, doing your own thing." The John Garfield social dropout was likely to be a hard drinker, a man of few and caustic words who despaired of finding a place for himself in a world of insensitive clods. In *Easy Rider* the hero or heroes (since the Dennis Hopper and Jack Nicholson characters are also searching for America) are now pot smoking, inarticulate types. But they're still looking for the same place, and in the strong tradition of romantic fiction they too are, of course, doomed to fail.

It may be that *Easy Rider* was the first hero-less movie, since many youngsters identified with the mood and philosophy and not with any of the characters. In fact, some critics felt that neither the Fonda nor Hopper character was a hero to youth. That the closest character to a "hero" they might find in the film would be Jack Nicholson.

In any case, the impact of the film, and its three leading players, was extraordinary and undeniable. *Easy Rider* changed the course of filmmaking for the 1970s.

Peter Fonda as filmmaker.

10
The Future of the Rebel Hero

As discussed in the foreword, this book has dealt with rebel hero stars and the characters they have portrayed. Over the years there have been many stars (Robert Mitchum, Kirk Douglas, Burt Lancaster, the late Alan Ladd, Clint Eastwood, Burt Reynolds and others) who possessed the personal qualities to have gained acceptance as rebel heroes but were never starred in appropriate "rebel" roles.

One young actor of the late sixties and early seventies who might be considered a rebel hero is Christopher Jones. He starred in two commercially successful films for American-International in which he displayed poten-

tial for rebel hero stardom. In *Wild in the Streets* he played an LSD pusher who becomes a rock and roll entertainer and eventually President of the United States. In that film all citizens over thirty-five, including his mother (played by Shelley Winters), were sent to compulsory "retirement" camps where they were kept on a steady diet of hallucinatory drugs.

Proving the importance of timing, a few years before *Wild in the Streets* Universal had released *Privilege*, an excellent British made film with a similar theme—a rock and roll idol who is manipulated into a political force. But the public wasn't yet ready to accept the theme.

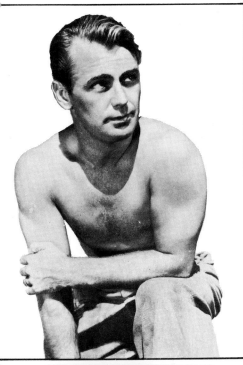

Some might-have-been rebel heroes: Alan Ladd, Sterling Hayden, Kirk Douglas, Burt Lancaster. Some yet may be rebels: George Peppard, Clint Eastwood, Burt Reynolds and rock singer James Taylor.

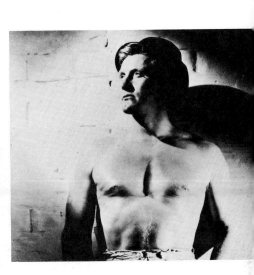

Chris Jones.

Christopher Jones as the rock and roll singing star who becomes President of the United States, in *Wild in the Streets*.

Christopher Jones in *Wild in the Streets*.

Christopher Jones, Shelley Winters.
Mother and son in *Wild in the Streets*.

Youth takes over politically in *Wild in the Streets*.

Christopher Jones, Judy Pace in *Three in the Attic*.

Christopher Jones, Yvette Mimieux in *Three in the Attic*.

Christopher Jones, Yvette Mimieux
in *Three in the Attic*

Although *Wild in the Streets* was not widely accepted by the older generation, the film was recognized by perceptive critics. "One of the most provocative and interesting movies to come out of Hollywood factories in a long time," said Judith Crist. Renata Adler in *The New York Times* called it "by far the best American film of the year . . . and a brutally witty and intelligent film."

Jones, as expected, was compared to James Dean. Archer Winsten said, "Chris Jones does look a very great deal like James Dean and acts like him too."

Although the film was a moderate box-office success and was enthusiastically received by the critics, Jones did not click with audiences and he did not have the "overnight" impact of Dean or Hoffman.

Three in the Attic followed, and *Newsweek* sarcastically reported, "Once again American-International Pictures breaks new ground and manures it thoroughly. The studio that gave the world *The Wild Angels* and *Wild in the Streets* is now investigating, with its customary scholarship, the phenomena of gang rape and female supremacy. 'You've heard of the sexual revolution?' asks Christopher Jones at the beginning of *Three in the Attic*. 'Well, I'm one of its first casualties.' "

The story concerned a young college student carrying on three simultaneous love affairs. The three girls meet, decide to teach him a lesson and lock him in an attic. They intend to sap and then destroy his sexual appetite.

The film received disastrous reviews and again Jones was labeled, this time by *San Francisco Chronicle* critic John L. Wasserman, "the poor man's James Dean." *Variety* agreed that Jones seemed prone to emulate Dean.

Jones went to Columbia for *The Looking Glass War*, another critical and box-office disappointment, and *Brief Season*.

While some of his films have been commercial if not critical successes, even after five films Jones has not "clicked" with audiences and hasn't yet achieved the status of a Dean, Newman, McQueen, Beatty, Fonda or Hoffman.

Jones has not had the career "advantage" of having his personal life highly publicized. But, despite the Dean comparisons, he possesses the screen qualities and talent to be a rebel hero star. In the seventies, he may yet achieve that position.

Robert Redford, who scored heavily in *Butch Cassidy and the Sundance Kid* and in his own production, *Downhill Racer*, also completed *Little Fauss and Big Halsey*, a film about the motorcycle cult in America. Even now, almost twenty years after *The Wild One*, motorcycle gangs are still the subjects of films about sub-culture heroes. Motorcycles are still the symbol of being beat, hippie, bohemian, someone alienated from the comfortable American way of life, someone trying to find himself on the roads of America.

Christopher Jones in *Brief Season*.

Christopher Jones, Pia Degermark in *The Looking Glass War*.

Robert Redford may be one of
the super-rebels of the seventies.

Michael J. Pollard, Robert Redford in *Little Fauss and Big Halsey*.

As big a rebel off-screen as McQueen, Beatty and Fonda, and the recipient of voluminous personal publicity, Redford also possesses the on-screen qualities to become a rebel hero star.

America's super off-screen rebel of the late sixties, football star Joe Namath, entered the running as a rebel hero in films with a starring role in C. C. & Co., another motorcycle epic, but the film was not a hit.

However, Namath's impact as a significant symbol of man vs. the system has even been discussed by political columnist James Reston in The New York Times. Reston described real-life Namath as the new anti-hero.

In 1970, another trend-setting film with non-conventional heroes was *M.A.S.H.* Although Donald Sutherland got top billing, it was Elliott Gould with this film (and the success of his previous picture, *Bob and Carol and Ted and Alice*) who scored with audiences and showed the potential for rebel hero stardom. In his case too, he received much personal publicity as an offbeat character (and husband of super-star Barbra Streisand), which intrigued audiences and led to his acceptance as an unconventional "hero."

Established actors like Redford, Jones and Gould may be the rebel hero stars of the seventies. And of course a

Dyan Cannon, Elliott Gould in
Bob and Carol and Ted and Alice.

Elliott Gould, Natalie Wood
between takes on
Bob and Carol and Ted and Alice.

new rebel hero star could emerge "overnight," á la Garfield, Dean, and Hoffman. While Christopher Jones, Elliott Gould, and Robert Redford have been given the opportunity of catching on as rebel heroes, there are additional rising young stars who possess the charisma and qualifications for rebel hero stardom. Rock star James Taylor is making his film debut this year in *Two-Lane Blacktop*. If he clicks in movies the way he has on records, he could become a new star and possible rebel hero material.

Perhaps the most exciting established actor with rebel hero potential is Burt Reynolds. Reynolds possesses the on-screen charisma and off-screen rebel qualifications for rebel hero stardom, including the "must" requirements of animal sex appeal and masculine good looks. In addition, he possesses an extra ingredient, a wry sense of humor, which may make him a new strain of screen rebel.

When asked if great sex appeal is vital to a rebel's success, Reynolds candidly answered: "Great sex appeal is important to *anything*. Even if you sell shirts. Because no matter what anybody says, it's really where the button is. No matter what *anybody* says."

Elliott Gould,, Candice Bergen in *Getting Straight*.

Gould, as a returnee to College, gets caught up in the new revolution. *Getting Straight*.

Reynolds has definite opinions about whether a rebel on-screen must be a rebel off-screen to succeed. "Yes, it helps. I think McQueen's off-screen image is fantastic. But that's what it is. An image. I think it's the greatest PR work in the world. And it works for him. Because men as well as women dig him. And I think it wouldn't hurt if I captured a bank robber running down Madison Avenue and threw him through a window. I think it would help, as a matter of fact. But if you have the right kind of properties—if I did *Butch Cassidy and the Sundance Kid*—it wouldn't matter if I played with Yo Yo's off-camera."

The right property and the right audience are the two greatest requirements for the emergence of a new

Mike Douglas, Kirk's son,
may be a future rebel hero of the screen.

Off-screen rebel hero football star
Joe Namath is trying to score in movies.
He seems to possess the necessary
qualifications for wide audience acceptance.

rebel. However, heroes are no longer clearly defined. It appears that the hero of the future will be a combination of all the heroes that the screen has known.

The future of the rebel hero as we have known him is unpredictable, since most films of this decade will be made about non-conventional heroes. But this does not mean that the rebel hero character will not reappear.

Currently, the day of the hero, indeed the day of the "star," seems over. But the motion picture industry is cyclical, and stars and heroes may again be necessary. Since dissent, protest, rebellion and alienation are an integral part of our society, the rebel hero in films, in one form or another, will survive.

Burt Reynolds

James Taylor